THE INTERMEDIA
REVISED AND E

SEATTLE COOKBOOK

BY JOHN OWEN

Illustrated by Alice Owen

The cover: Pike Place Market Morning by Alice Owen

Other Cookbooks by John Owen

Intermediate Eater
Second Intermediate Eater
Gourmand Gutbusters
The Great Grub Hunt
The Seattle Cookbook
    First Edition 1983
    Second Edition 1985
    Third Edition 1993

P-I Books
From the Seattle Post-Intelligencer

Copyright, 1993
Seattle Post-Intelligencer
Seattle, Washington

ISBN 0-9624559-1-1

TABLE OF CONTENTS

ESPRESSO ON THE BAY

COFFEE CAKES & BREAD

ESPRESSO ON THE BAY

I don't know whether it's a comment on the Seattle weather or the civic psyche. But this may be the only city in the world where a sign hanging over the corner gas station reads:

Coffee 60 cents.

Espresso $1.25.

Latte $1.50.

Whatever happened to regular, unleaded and diesel?

Maybe the attendants are weary of changing the numbers according to the latest bulletins from the Middle East. Or perhaps they are merely reflecting the passions of their customers. Face it, nobody gets very excited about gasoline in Seattle.

But, boy, are the residents serious about their morning cup of coffee.

The giant buried fuel tanks don't contain high-octane any more. They're all filled with espresso. You can operate a service station in Seattle without an air pump, a pair of pliers or a ball peen hammer. But you'd better know how to create a racehorse (four shots of espresso) or a tall skinny (latte with non-fat milk.)

The customers fill their cars up once a week. But they fill themselves up with espresso on the hour. In front of most service stations espresso carts have replaced jump-start battery wagons. In a way, they serve the same function.

Such is the consumption rate along Puget Sound that freighters from South and Central America will soon be jamming the channels leading through the Straits of Juan de Fuca. Inevitably there is bound to be a "coffee spill" in Elliott Bay. And a coffee pipeline between West Seattle and the Juan Valdez plantation will be proposed.

The last time I checked, the Seattle Yellow Pages listed 161 coffee companies, houses or firms selling coffee machines or dispensers. And that doesn't include the espresso stands that have sprouted up and down our avenues like mushrooms in a cow pasture.

When the Super Bowl game was in Florida, we patronized a coffee vendor in the financial district of Tampa. He told us he was pioneering street sales of quality coffee in that city. His goal, he said, was to create the kind of awareness and appreciation the people of Seattle have achieved. When we told him we were from the Emerald City the vendor instinctively genuflected. The Pope doesn't get a better reception at a Knights of Columbus clambake.

In fact the Pope wouldn't believe the scene which is re-enacted every rainy weekend morning at a popular neighborhood coffee shop like Veneto's in Bellevue. People come stumbling in from four directions wearing bathrobes, jogging suits, designer grubbies. Their eyes are thin slits, their teeth clenched, their hands trembling.

Ten minutes later they are laughing, carousing, telling ribald jokes, slapping each other on their bottoms. You'd swear they'd each mainlined a quart of Geritol.

That's life by the old coffee pump in Seattle. And here's what you are supposed to eat with your cup of java.

JAVA GINGERBREAD

2 1/2 cups sifted flour
2 teaspoons baking soda
1/2 teaspoon salt
1 teaspoon cinnamon
1 1/2 teaspoons powdered ginger
1/2 teaspoon powdered cloves
1/2 teaspoon dry mustard
1/2 teaspoon black pepper
1 cube butter
1/2 cup brown sugar, firmly packed
2 eggs
1 cup molasses
1 rounded tablespoon instant coffee
1 cup boiling water

Preheat the oven to 375°. Grease a 9-inch square pan and dust lightly with fine, dry bread crumbs.

Sift together the flour, baking soda, salt, cinnamon, ginger, cloves, mustard and black pepper and set all this aside.

In the large bowl of your Mixmaster cream the softened butter. Add the sugar and beat two minutes. Beat in the eggs one at a time, using a spatula occasionally to run down the sides. You can use a metal spoon instead, but the Mixmaster will likely use it as a 5-inch shell to shoot a hole through your kitchen wall.

Add the molasses and beat again until smooth.

Dissolve the coffee in the boiling water. On low speed dump into the mess resting in your Mixmaster bowl the dry ingredients, a third at a time. Slurp in half a cup of coffee and when that disappears glunk in the rest.

When you have a smooth, thin puddle in your bowl shut off the mixer and pour the sludge into the waiting pan. Bake on the center rack of the oven for about 35 minutes.

Remove pan and let the bread cool for 10 minutes. Remove to a rack and you can serve it in squares or slices after it has cooled. Better yet, serve while it's still warm with whipped cream or a dollop of vanilla ice cream.

CHEESE BREAD

1 loaf French bread, sliced
1 jar processed American cheese
1/2 teaspoon garlic salt
1 teaspoon marjoram
1 tablespoon sesame seeds
1/4 cup chopped parsley
3 tablespoons sherry

Spread the bread slices with the mess created by mixing the last six ingredients. Wrap the loaf in foil and heat in a 325° oven for 30 minutes.

BANANA CARROT BREAD

1/2 stick butter, softened
3/4 cup sugar
2 large eggs
1 cup very ripe banana, mashed
2 cups sifted flour
2 teaspoons double-acting baking powder
1/2 teaspoon cinnamon
1/2 teaspoon salt
1/4 teaspoon baking soda
1/8 teaspoon ground cloves
1 cup chopped pecans
3/4 cup grated carrot
1 teaspoon vanilla

Cream together the butter and sugar until light and fluffy. Beat in the eggs, one at a time. When thoroughly combined stir in the mashed banana.

In another bowl sift together the flour, baking powder, cinnamon, salt, baking soda and cloves.

Stir the flour mixture into the banana mixture (wow, aren't we having fun?) and add the pecans, grated carrot and vanilla. Combine the batter well and pour into a well-buttered loaf pan, 9 by 5 inches. Bake in a preheated 350° oven for an hour.

Let cool in the pan 20 minutes and then turn out onto a rack and let cool completely.

COFFEETOWN CORNBREAD

1 1/2 cups unsifted flour
2 tablespoons baking powder
1/4 cup sugar
1 teaspoon salt
1 1/2 cups yellow cornmeal
1/3 cup grated Parmesan cheese
1/3 cup chopped green pepper
1/4 cup chopped green onions
6 tablespoons melted butter or margarine
4 teaspoons chili powder
1 1/3 cups milk
2 slightly beaten eggs

Sift together the flour, baking powder, sugar and salt. Stir in the cornmeal, Parmesan, green pepper and green onion.

In a bowl mix the milk, eggs, chili powder and melted butter. Glunk this mess into the dry ingredients all at once, stir just until blended, then pour batter into a well-greased 9-inch square cake pan.

Bake the cornbread at 400° for 35 minutes or until it survives the Old Toothpick Test. Serve hot.

This cornbread is also good split and toasted for breakfast. Better not have an extra piece, though. Your ferry is scheduled to leave ... two minutes ago.

CHEESE POPOVERS

1 cup unsifted flour
1/2 teaspoon chili powder
1/8 teaspoon cayenne pepper
1/4 teaspoon garlic salt
1/2 teaspoon salt
1 tablespoon melted butter
1 cup milk
3 eggs
1 cup shredded sharp cheddar cheese

Preheat oven to 375°. Combine the first six ingredients in an electric mixer bowl. Add the butter, milk and eggs and beat about three minutes. Stir in the cheese.

Divide the batter into about a dozen cups of a well-greased muffin pan. Each cup should be slightly more than half full.

Bake 45-50 minutes and serve hot.

BLUE CORN MUFFINS

1 1/2 cups flour
1 cup blue cornmeal
1 tablespoon baking powder
1/2 teaspoon salt
1 1/2 teaspoons sugar
1 1/2 cups milk
2 eggs, beaten lightly
1/4 cup canola oil

You can find blue cornmeal in the larger super-markets and in food specialty shops. Combine a cup of the cornmeal with the flour, baking powder, salt and sugar. Add the milk, eggs and oil and stir just until everything is wet.

Spoon this mess into well-buttered muffin tins about three-quarters full. Bake in the middle of a 400° oven for 15 to 17 minutes. Let muffins cool two minutes then turn out on a rack.

TORTILLA STICKS

Dip flour tortillas in water. When drained of excess fluid but still wet, sprinkle grated Parmesan cheese over one side of each tortilla and roll into an inch-round cylinder (with the cheese inside). Fasten with a toothpick so it will hold its shape. Lightly sprinkle the outside of the tortillas with salt.

Or you can skip the salt.

Place on a greased baking sheet and shove into a preheated 500° oven, about four minutes on each side. But watch carefully so you don't burn 'em.

You want the tortilla sticks (with toothpicks removed) golden brown and warm.

CRANBANANA BREAD

2 cups fresh cranberries
1 cup sugar
3/4 cup water
1/3 cup shortening
2/3 cup sugar
2 eggs
1 3/4 cups sifted flour
1/2 teaspoon salt
2 teaspoons baking powder
1/4 teaspoon baking soda
1/2 cup chopped walnuts
1 cup mashed ripe banana

Moosh together the cranberries, sugar and water. Boil five to 10 minutes, until berries pop. Drain and measure to make one cup of berries.

Cream together the shortening and sugar. Add the eggs one at a time, beating well. Sift into this mess the flour, salt, baking powder and soda. Add alternately the bananas and nuts. Mix everything together with the dipstick from a 1947 Hudson, folding in the cranberries as the final ingredient.

Pour into a greased 9-by-5-inch loaf pan. Bake in a preheated 350° oven for 45 to 60 minutes.

If you want it glazed, boil 1 1/4 cups of sugar with 1/4 cup of water until slightly syrupy. Spread on the hot bread and let cool.

COFFEE CART MUFFINS

2 cups whole wheat flour
1 tablespoon baking powder
1 teaspoon cinnamon
3/4 teaspoon salt
2 eggs
3/4 cup milk
1/3 cup oil
1/4 cup honey
1 cup coarsely grated zucchini
2/3 cup raisins

What you do is to oil the muffin cups, sift together the dry ingredients and in another bowl beat the eggs and mix with the oil, milk and honey. Add the dry ingredients but stir just to moisten. Stir in the zucchini and raisins and spoon that gloop into the muffin cups. Bake 20 to 25 minutes in a 375° oven.

PIKE PLACE MARKET

SALADS

PIKE PLACE MARKET

Our guided tour through the Pike Place Market was interrupted by one of the Muscatel Musketeers, who tried to sell a potted geranium to a woman in our group. He did not explain how the posy had come into his possession. It was obviously better not to ask.

When the woman declined the opportunity for a cash purchase, the man with the geranium growing out of his hand reached a snap decision.

"Tell you what I'm going to do," he announced grandly. "You're still half-pretty. I'm gonna give you this flower!"

That's one way you might describe the Pike Place Market. It's old, but still half-pretty. Several years ago some well-intentioned but misguided civic busybodies tried to slap some rouge and mascara on the old girl to cover up the warts. But sanity prevailed. Pig's trotters, kippered herring, geoducks, skate wings, quail eggs, crab claws, parsnips, sweet onions, garlic ropes, lutefisk. That adds up to a "10." But the Pike Place Market is no beauty queen.

The locals still treasure it, for a Saturday shopping excursion, a walking lunch on a business day or for the fine dining opportunities stretching from Il Bistro on Pike past the Athenian to Cutter's at the other end, on Western Avenue.

In the summer you can dine Italian on the terrace at the almost hidden Pink Door. In the winter you can find cold beer and a warm greeting inside Kells Irish Restaurant and Pub.

The Pike Place Market also has a first rate art stall right next to DeLaurenti's Italian grocery. Alice the Artist and the other art stall members serve as informal information booth attendants and report that the first three questions they used to be asked by tourists were:

"Where's the rest room?"

"Where can I get some fish and chips?"

And, "How do I get to the waterfront from here?"

In recent years, a new question has moved to the top of the list.

"Where are the flying fish?"

"Take a right at the flower stall," the artists reply. "When you see a tourist kid posing for a photo while sitting on top of a giant pig, you're just about there."

"There" is the Pike Place Fish Market, where the vendors treat silver salmon like Seahawk footballs, floating them through the air from ice bin to the counter scale. Unlike the Seahawks, the fish vendors almost never fumble or throw an incompletion.

The market didn't have a show-stopping act like this when it opened back in 1907. H. O. Blanchard sold the first produce on Pike Street. Nobody remembers the initial item purchased but since Blanchard hailed from Renton Junction he probably didn't unload a lot of mangoes, papayas or ash trays made out of Mount St. Helen's ash.

Blanchard sold his produce off the back of a horse-drawn wagon. These days market wares are sold off low stalls, high stalls, specialty shops and by a roaming benefactor who can still make you a helluva price on a potted flower, provided you're still half-pretty.

The "low stalls" are just that, built about three feet off the ground and occupied by truck farmers who sell only the fresh produce they grow. The high stalls — with the pineapples and mushrooms and the oranges arranged so an avalanche will break your wrist if you touch a single one — are permanent produce stands.

The specialty shops offer everything from goat's milk to English crumpets to tortilla presses or sausage casings to filo dough, fresh linguini, Turkish coffee and jalapeno jelly. Some of the best craft items in the Northwest can be found at the booths, which are rebuilt in the early hours of each morning.

PIKE PLACE PEA SALAD

1 1/4 cups fresh or frozen peas
1/4 cup sliced green onions, including tops
1/4 cup shredded carrot
1/2 cup shredded cabbage
1/4 cup salad oil
2 tablespoons wine vinegar
1 tablespoon catsup
1 teaspoon sugar
1/4 teaspoon garlic salt
1/4 teaspoon dry basil
1/4 teaspoon freshly ground black pepper

Cook the peas in boiling water just until barely tender. Combine with the onion, carrot and cabbage in a salad bowl. In a cup mix the other ingredients, slop over the veggies, stir well, cover and refrigerate for a couple of hours.

PASTA PEPPER SALAD

1/2 pound bowtie noodles or shell macaroni
1 bunch broccoli
3 red peppers
2 cans albacore tuna, 7 ounces each

Peel the broccoli stems and cut into half-inch slices. Whack the flowered part into hunks about an inch in size. Steam the stems and flowerettes separately and when barely tender run under cold water, then pat dry.

Discard the stem portion, white pith and seeds from the red peppers and cut into inch-square hunks.

Cook the pasta in boiling salted water until just tender to the bite. Drain and cool.

In a salad bowl combine the pasta and peppers. Add the broccoli and the salad dressing described below. Add the tuna in chunks, toss again lightly, let chill for an hour or two and then serve to four to six guests, depending upon their capacity, along with French bread and white wine.

THE DRESSING

1/2 cup olive oil
2 tablespoons red wine vinegar
2 tablespoons drained capers
1 teaspoon oregano leaves, crumbled
3/4 teaspoon salt
1/2 teaspoon minced garlic
1/4 teaspoon ground pepper

Mix together and add to salad as described above.

COLD CHICKEN SALAD

1 fryer chicken
1 cup chopped celery
1/2 cup pitted and halved black olives
3 green onions, chopped
1 tablespoon lemon juice
1/3 cup walnuts
salt, pepper
basil mayonnaise (recipe below)

What you do is to bring a large pot of salted water to a boil, plop in the chicken, cover, let simmer 15 minutes, shut off the heat and let the clucker do the backstroke in the covered pot for another hour.

Remove chicken, separate the meat from the skin and bones, which should be discarded, along with all that bad language you used while juggling the hot chicken.

Chop the chicken meat when cool and mix with the chopped celery, olives, chopped onions and the walnuts. Sprinkle with lemon juice and add salt and pepper to taste.

Moisten with some of the basil mayonnaise, dish up four helpings on plates holding a leaf or two of lettuce, glunk some more mayonnaise on top of the salad and serve. Oh, yeah, you want to know how to construct some green glunk, right?

BASIL MAYONNAISE

1 1/2 cups olive or canola oil
1 cup fresh basil leaves
1/2 cup celery leaves
1 egg
1 tablespoon Dijon mustard
3 tablespoons lemon juice
2 cloves garlic, smashed
1/4 teaspoon salt
1/4 teaspoon ground ginger

Dump in the blender a cup of the oil plus the basil and celery leaves. Whir until the leaves are chopped then pour this sludge into a bowl.

Now plop into the uncleaned blender the egg, mustard, garlic, lemon juice, salt and ginger. Punch the button again, and when the machine is whirring nicely slowly pour through the top of the blender opening the one-quarter remaining cup of oil, very, very slowly.

When it has all been absorbed, add in small blobs the basil oil mixture, while the blender is still running. When it has all been mixed in and absorbed you are ready to add it to the chicken salad.

LOUIE'S SEAFOOD SALAD SAUCE

1 cup mayonnaise
1/2 cup chili sauce
1 teaspoon sage
1 small clove garlic, minced
1/4 teaspoon salt
dash of nutmeg
grinding of pepper
1 tablespoon minced onion
1 tablespoon minced green pepper
1 tablespoon capers

Blend the first seven ingredients together. Then mix in the green pepper, onion and capers.

This should be ample sauce for at least four seafood salad servings. Mix crab meat, shrimp or a combination of the two with chopped celery, hard-boiled eggs and pitted black olives then goop the gloop over the top.

SNOQUALMIE VALLEY SLAW

2 cups shredded cabbage
1 cup chopped celery
1 cup chopped onion
1 green pepper, chopped fine
2 tablespoons salad oil
3 tablespoons vinegar
3 tablespoons sugar
1/2 teaspoon pepper
1 teaspoon salt
1/4 teaspoon garlic powder

Mix the cabbage, celery, onion and green pepper in a large bowl. Gloop everything else together in a small bowl. Pour small bowl into large bowl, and you have a slug of slaw.

SOUTH PARK SPINACH SALAD

1 head lettuce
1 bunch spinach
1 tablespoon butter
1/2 cup sesame seeds
1/4 cup Parmesan cheese
4 slices cooked bacon, crumbled
1 cup sour cream
1 tablespoon white wine vinegar
1 tablespoon sugar
1/4 cup chopped green pepper
1 green onion, chopped
1/2 teaspoon salt
1/4 teaspoon garlic salt

All you do is break the lettuce into bite-sized chunks; tear the spinach leaves and place in a salad bowl with the lettuce. Melt the butter in a small pan and lightly brown the sesame seeds. Cool, add the grated Parmesan cheese and the crumbled bacon. Add to the greens.

Combine the sour cream, vinegar, sugar, green pepper, onion, salt and garlic salt. Pour over the greens, toss lightly and that will serve eight to 10.

SARKOWSKY SALAD

1/2 pound sliced fresh mushrooms
1 avocado, peeled and diced
1 zucchini, thinly sliced
1 tomato, diced
1/4 cup sliced scallions
1 teaspoon sugar
1 teaspoon salt
1/2 teaspoon ground black pepper
1/2 teaspoon marjoram leaves, crumbled
4 tablespoons salad oil
2 tablespoons wine vinegar
lettuce leaves

Herman Sarkowsky, local business and sports figure, says to mix together the mushrooms, avocado, zucchini, tomato and scallions. Sprinkle this mess with sugar, salt, pepper and marjoram and toss. Then add the oil and vinegar, toss again until well-coated and serve to six guests on lettuce-lined salad plates.

HOT CHICKEN SALAD

cooked meat from one fryer
1 cup diced celery
1 cup chopped walnuts
3/4 cup mayonnaise
2 tablespoons chopped green onion
1/2 teaspoon salt
1/4 teaspoon pepper
2 tablespoons chopped green pepper
3 boiled eggs, chopped
1 tablespoon lemon juice
1 can cream of chicken soup
2 cups crushed potato chips

Cook the chicken according to the same formula used in the cold chicken salad recipe in this chapter. Mix the chicken meat with all the ingredients except the soup and potato chips.

Spread this mess over the bottom of a flat oven baking dish. Pour the undiluted soup over the top, sprinkle with the potato chips and shove into a 425° oven for 20 minutes.

WOODLAND PARK ZOO

SOUP

WOODLAND PARK ZOO

With the addition of an elephant complex and a tropical rain forest it has reestablished its reputation as one of the country's top zoos. But I'm not sure you should take the kids to Woodland Park.

Oh, sure, there is a great kiddie area with lots of touchable fuzzies. Nearby there's a five-acre African savanna with lions and giraffes separated from each other, and from us, by concealed fences and moats preserving the look of a free-run game range in Kenya or Tarzania.

There are zebras and springboks, Egyptian geese and African whydahs, there are man-made ponds and rocks with built-in heating coils.

But I'm pretty sure the Woodland Park Zoo should carry an "X" rating. The place is a sex swamp!

Haven't you noticed the local zoologists' preoccupation with reproduction? Well, it's been going on since Bobo and Fifi were barely at the hand-holding stage in the Great Ape House. When were they going to start having babies, the public demanded to know. Good grief, Bobo didn't even have a steady job at the time, and Fifi was still convinced that baby apes dropped out of the feeding bin along with the bananas and cabbages.

The zookeepers insisted upon mating Tinkerbell to Toby the siamang ape when he was still going steady with a rubber tire.

And the newspapers in Seattle have, to be honest, helped foster the sensationalism of Woodland Park Zoo.

"Coco the sloth gives birth!" one headline trumpeted.

"Nina the gorilla pregnant again!" another harrumphed, as all the neighborhood harpies began counting the months.

The hippo honcho wrung his head in public view and bemoaned the lack of bedroom action involving Gertie and Kubwa Sana. Ruff the Kodiak bear couldn't even breathe into Fannie's ear without promoting loud applause from peeping toms. Alexandria and Nicolas were expected to phone in the news to gossip columnists, if they were expecting any little snow leopards.

The zoo people proclaimed that the lions were sexually hyperactive. And newspaper critics proclaimed Timba the Gorilla devoid of all feminine graces, when she arrived here for breeding purposes. Little wonder that Kiki plotted his escape from the gorilla enclosure, by employing a tree branch as a vaulting pole. He probably had an appointment with a sex therapist.

Like I said, it's a sex swamp. And matters would not be improved by the addition of a liquor license for zoo eating establishments, the object of frequent debate in the Woodland Park community. Serve a sloe gin fizz to a shaft-tailed whydah and she is liable to elope with a wart hog.

What they should be serving the animals at Woodland Park is hot soup, and if somebody throws a bone into your food trough you might use it to construct the soup on the next page.

Woodland Park Zoop

1 1/2 pounds ham hocks, sawed twice
3 onions, sliced
1 cup carrots, chopped
2 cloves garlic, minced
2 cups chopped celery, including leaves
2 teaspoons butter
1 1/2 cup dried split peas
12 peppercorns, smashed
1 bay leaf
1 teaspoon thyme
1 teaspoon oregano
1 teaspoon marjoram
6 cups chicken stock
1 cup evaporated milk
salt, pepper
dry sherry

Brown the ham hocks in butter melted in a large soup pot. Dump in the onions, carrots, garlic, celery, peas, smashed peppercorns, herbs and chicken stock. Bring to a boil, cover, lower heat and simmer for three hours. Remove ham hock and discard bay leaf.

Put the soup through a blender in batches, then return to the pot. Add the ham from the hocks, in hunks. Gloop in the evaporated milk, reheat and add salt, pepper and sherry to taste.

Mushroom Chicken Chowder

12 ounces fresh mushrooms, sliced
2 tablespoons canola oil
1/2 cup chopped onion
1/2 cup sliced celery
2 cups chicken broth
1 can whole tomatoes, run briefly through the blender
1 cup egg noodles
1/2 teaspoon salt
ground pepper
1 bay leaf
2 cups cooked chicken

Heat the oil in a pot and dump in the mushrooms, onions and celery and cook for about five minutes. Add the chicken broth, tomatoes, noodles, salt, pepper and bay leaf to simmer, covered, until the noodles are barely tender.

Remove the bay leaf, add the chicken and simmer another five minutes.

I have also used this recipe with the carcass from a used turkey, doubling all the other ingredients.

Emerald City Onion Soup

6 medium onions, sliced
1/3 cup olive oil
1/2 teaspoon pepper
1 1/2 teaspoons salt
1 teaspoon sugar
1/2 teaspoon thyme
4 bay leaves
1 clove garlic, minced
1 teaspoon caraway seeds
2 tablespoons steak sauce
2 quarts beef stock
1/2 cup dry white wine
toast or croutons
Swiss cheese

Saute the onion in olive oil until brown. Add the pepper, salt, sugar, spices and steak sauce. Simmer 10 minutes.

Glunk in the beef stock or bouillon and simmer for an hour. Add the white wine and boil 10 minutes.

Serve in large bowls, plunk a large crouton or round of toast on top of each, cover with grated cheese and shove under an oven broiler until melted.

Latona Lentil Soup

1/4 pound bacon, chopped
1 large onion, chopped
1 cup diced carrots
1 package (12 ounces) dried lentils
7 cups water
2 tablespoons red wine vinegar
6 beef bouillon cubes
1/2 teaspoon cinnamon
2 teaspoons dry mustard
1/3 cup catsup
1/2 pound kielbasa sausage

Cook the bacon until crisp in a large soup pot. Remove bacon, drain and reserve. To the fat in the pot add the onion and carrots and cook three or four minutes, stirring occasionally.

Wash the lentils thoroughly then dump into the pot along with the water, vinegar, bouillon, cinnamon, mustard and catsup. Bring to a boil then reduce heat and simmer, covered, for an hour. Add salt as needed.

Cut the kielbasa into chunks, add to the soup, let it simmer another 15 minutes and call the crowd for supper.

Meridian Broccoli Chowder

2 pounds fresh broccoli
24 ounces chicken broth
4 cups milk
1 cup minced ham
1 cup sliced mushrooms
1/2 pound Monterey jack cheese, shredded
1/4 teaspoon pepper

Cook the broccoli, covered, in half the broth until tender. Cool and chop coarsely and reserve.

Add to the pot the remaining broth, milk, ham (you can use the El Cheapo brand, thick-sliced and packaged variety if you're on a budget).

Add the cheese and broccoli, heat again, add salt to taste and this should make four to five big bowls.

Clam-Mushroom Bisque

3/4 pound fresh mushrooms, sliced
3 tablespoons butter
1 tablespoon flour
2 cups heated clam nectar
1/3 cup cream
salt, pepper to taste

Saute the sliced mushrooms in the melted butter until barely tender. Reduce heat to low and sprinkle with the flour, then stir everything together.

Add the nectar in a stream and simmer five minutes. Moosh everything in a blender, then return to the pan. Add the cream and seasonings and this will serve two to three.

Cathlamet Crab Bisque

3 tablespoons butter
3 tablespoons flour
1 1/2 quarts half and half
1 teaspoon salt
1/2 teaspoon white pepper
6 ounces crab meat
1/2 cup dry sherry

Melt the butter in the top of a double boiler, stir in the flour and stir-cook for about three minutes. Glunk in the half and half, salt and pepper and stir-cook until the bisque has thickened.

Add the crab meat and sherry, reheat and this will provide four main-dish servings or six, first-course portions.

Green Lake Cabbage Soup

4 tablespoons butter
1 medium-large head cabbage
2 chopped onions
2 tablespoons flour
6 cups water
6 chicken bouillon cubes
1 pound can of tomatoes
2 tablespoons lemon juice
2 tablespoons sugar
1/2 teaspoon pepper
1/2 teaspoon caraway seeds

Melt the butter in a big pot. Core and chop the cabbage and toss into the pot along with the peeled and diced onion. Stir-cook this for about 15 minutes.

Sprinkle with flour, stirring into the cabbage mixture. Run the tomatoes through the blender and dump them into the pot along with all the other ingredients and simmer for an hour.

Fremont Minestrone

3 tablespoons olive oil
2 cups chopped onion
1/2 pound Italian sausage
8 cups beef stock
1 tablespoon dried basil (or 2 tablespoons fresh)
1 clove garlic, minced
1/4 teaspoon black pepper
pinch of cayenne pepper
1/2 teaspoon salt
3 cups diced potatoes
1/2 cup tiny pasta seashells
4 cups fresh spinach

You can eliminate the sausage for a vegetarian meal. Or you can go for the whole ball of wax and remove the sausage from the casing, crumble into a pan, cook until browned, pour off the grease and reserve the meat.

In your large soup pot saute the onion in olive oil. When the onion is soft dump in the sausage, beef broth, chopped basil, garlic, black and red pepper, salt and the potatoes. Cover the pot, let liquid come to a simmer and cook for 10 minutes.

Add the seashell pasta to the pot, cover and cook another six minutes or until it is done. Tear the spinach by hand, toss it into the pot and when the stock returns to a simmer remove from the heat and serve the soup along with freshly grated Parmesan.

Sixty-Sixth Street Soup

2 carrots
1 potato
1 onion
1 turnip
1 celery stalk with leaves
1 tablespoon butter
6 tablespoons dried split peas
1/2 teaspoon black pepper
1/2 teaspoon nutmeg
1 teaspoon basil
1 whole clove
2 cloves garlic
ham bone
3 ounces noodles
2 1/2 quarts water

You can use a couple of ham hocks if you don't have a meaty ham bone. Or you can eliminate the ham altogether and use chicken broth instead of water.

Peel the carrots, potato, onion and turnip and cut the vegetables into inch-sized hunks. Melt the butter in a large pot and dump in the vegetables. Cook for five minutes, then add the split peas, the ham bone, all of the seasonings and the crushed cloves of garlic. Add the water and noodles and let simmer for 2 1/2 hours.

Let the soup cool a bit and remove the bone and any hunks of ham. Puree the rest of the soup, in batches in a blender. Add pieces of ham, reheat the soup in a pot, add salt to taste and serve up with some hot bread.

Bathhouse Bean Soup

1 pound black beans
1 chopped onion
1/2 cup chopped celery
10 cups beef stock
1 teaspoon minced garlic
1/4 cup sherry
1 teaspoon salt
black and cayenne pepper to taste
1 lemon

Soak the beans in water to cover overnight. Drain and rinse twice.

Heat some oil in your soup pot and saute the onion and celery. When they are softer than a gorilla's glance, add the beef stock and toss in the beans and garlic, too.

Simmer the soup for 2 1/2 hours. Puree in a blender and return to the pot. Add the sherry, salt, pepper and cayenne. Serve to the cast members of the Bathhouse Theater with a slice of lemon atop each bowl.

Rose Garden Bean Soup

1 pound small white beans
2 onions
2 cloves garlic
olive oil
1 1/2 teaspoon turmeric
1/2 teaspoon cayenne pepper
water
1 sawed hock or leftover ham bone
6 teaspoons chicken bouillon base
1 teaspoon sage
1 teaspoon pepper
1/2 teaspoon celery salt
instant potato buds

Soak the beans overnight.

Peel and chop the onions and garlic, toss into a large soup pot containing two tablespoons of hot olive oil. When the onion has softened add the turmeric and cayenne and stir-cook a minute.

Glunk in three quarts water, then add the drained beans, ham hock, bouillon, sage, pepper and celery salt. Simmer until the beans are tender but not mooshy.

Remove the ham bone and let the soup cool in the refrigerator. Skim off the fat and add the cooked ham in chunks. Reheat soup, add instant buds to thicken and add salt as needed.

A Bowl of Butternut

1 tablespoon butter
1 onion, chopped
3 cloves garlic, pressed
1 tablespoon chopped fresh ginger
5 cups butternut squash meat
5 cups chicken stock
pinch of sugar
1/4 cup fresh lime juice

Melt butter in soup pot. Dump in the onion, garlic and ginger and saute everything for about 20 minutes over medium-low heat, stirring once or twice.

Add to the pot the squash, stock and sugar. Bring to a boil, lower heat and simmer 20 minutes or until squash is tender. With a slotted spoon remove the solids from the pot, puree in a blender or processor, return to the pot and blend in with the stock. Reheat and add the lime juice. This makes about eight cups of soup.

THANKSGIVING SOUP

1 10-ounce can chicken broth
1 1/2 cups cubed potatoes
2 tablespoons butter or margarine
1/2 cup minced onion
1 10-ounce package frozen chopped broccoli
1/2 teaspoon mustard seed
1/2 teaspoon dillweed
2 cups milk
1 cup shredded Swiss cheese
salt

Cook the potatoes in chicken broth until tender, then run through a processor or food mill.

Melt butter in a soup pot. Add onion and saute until soft. Dump in mustard seed, dillweed and thawed broccoli. When broccoli is barely done, add the potato muck, milk and cheese. (It will melt more readily if you use processed Swiss cheese.) Salt to taste.

This should make about four bowls of soup. If you want it richer, use half and half instead of milk.

LOTS OF LENTIL

2 tablespoons canola oil
2 stalks celery, chopped
1 large onion, chopped
1 large carrot, chopped
1 tablespoon flour
2 quarts beef stock
2 cups lentils
2 bay leaves
2 whole cloves
1/2 teaspoon ground cumin
4 frankfurters, sliced
1/4 cup cider vinegar

If you want to add a little flavor (and fat) to this dish, dice a 1/4 pound of bacon and fry until lightly browned in soup pot, then proceed as indicated below. If you want a low-fat soup, use the canola for your browning oil.

Saute the celery, onion and carrot in the canola or bacon fat until tender. Stir in the flour, then add the washed lentils, the cumin and the beef stock.

Add the bay leaves and cloves. You can wrap and tie them in a bit of cheesecloth or put into a tea ball and drop that in the soup.

Bring the soup to a boil, reduce heat and simmer two hours. Discard the spices.

Scoop up some of the lentils in a strainer and then with a wooden spoon press the pulp through the screen back into the soup, to thicken.

Add the sliced frankfurters and vinegar. This will serve six to eight. If you let the soup sit awhile, it may thicken. Just add a bit of hot water to thin.

VEG-A-NOODLE SOUP

5 cups soup stock
1 thinly sliced onion
2 cloves garlic, minced
1 tablespoon ginger root, minced
1 tablespoon soy sauce
1 carrot, cut in julienne
2 cups red cabbage, shredded
1 cup sliced fresh mushrooms
2 cups fresh bean sprouts
handful of fresh pea pods
1/2 cup of dry noodles

You can use more noodles if you wish, but if so they should be cooked in water first, so they don't soak up all the soup stock. And if you use cooked noodles they should be added at the last minute. (You can now buy inexpensive eggless noodles in most supermarkets.)

You can use chicken or vegetable stock, as you prefer. You should always have some ginger root in your refrigerator. Peel it, shove it into a small jar, fill with sherry and it will keep for approximately 17 1/2 years.

All you do is simmer the onion, garlic and ginger in a cup of the stock until the onion softens. Add the rest of the stock and the soy, bring to a low boil and add the remaining ingredients in the order listed. As soon as the noodles have softened the veggies should be done, but still crisp.

Dish up into four bowls (or two big ones if this is your main course) and add more soy sauce to your taste.

ORZO SOUP

2 tablespoons oil or butter
1 Spanish onion, chopped
2 stalks celery, diced
2 carrots, peeled and diced
10 cups chicken broth
1 tablespoon fresh (or 1 teaspoon dried) each of marjoram, rosemary and thyme
1/2 cup orzo
1 pound raw, boneless, skinned chicken breasts

Heat the oil or butter in a soup pot on low heat, add the veggies and cook about 15 minutes, stirring occasionally. Add the stock, herbs, bring to a boil, add the orzo, reduce heat to low again and cook uncovered one hour.

Add the raw chicken breast meat in hunks. (Actually, I prefer an equivalent amount of chicken thigh meat.) Simmer until done. It will take about 20 minutes for breasts, slightly longer for thigh meat.

Cool, skim off the fat, reheat and serve.

GASWORKS PARK

CHILI

GASWORKS PARK

It seems only fitting that Gasworks Park once served as the site of the Seattle chili championships. Matter of fact, the event was held in the old boiler house.

Even before that, mere mention of the site gave some of our city fathers acid indigestion. They clearly thought that architect Rich Haag had marbles in his holding tank when he announced that the park would be built around six ancient cracking towers.

"Right," they said, looking curiously at the architect. "Cracking towers."

"I'm also planning a play barn in the gas exhauster building," he added brightly. "The kids can climb all over the engines, pumps and flywheels."

"Weren't you the playground director at Three Mile Island before you took this gig?" skeptics were inclined to ask.

Well, not only is Gasworks Park a recreational success, Haag received a national award from HUD for the design, "which transformed an urban blight into a center of beauty." For once, Uncle Sam wasn't just whistling through his beard.

One recent Sunday we spotted 26 kites and 43 sailboats from the hill that overlooks Lake Union. It probably should have been dedicated as Mount Crud since it was built upon 35,000 yards of tar, benzene and oil-soaked soil which was bulldozed into a giant mound, then buried under topsoil and grass.

Today, on the east shore of Lake Union, there are houseboat "lots" which have sold for $100,000 and up. Why? The answer is obvious. They afford a great view of six cracking towers and Mount Crud.

As for Lake Union, well, it was originally called Kah Chug (Little Waters) by the local Indians but was renamed by Thomas Mercer who could foresee the day when the body of water would provide a "union" between Lake Washington and Puget Sound. He suggested the new title at a lakeside picnic of early Seattle settlers. They probably served venison chili, generating the first measurable steam north of Henry Yesler's sawmill.

Gasworks Park is just one of several colorful sites where the region's chili heads congregate for indigestion competition.

They set up tents, lean-tos, giant umbrellas and even in a rain storm the chili team members insist they are having a helluva time. Which suggests there has to be something in those jugs of theirs besides jalapeno sauce.

The teams are often motivated by their lust for bonus points. Get enough points at various chili contests across the Northwest and you qualify to enter the World Chili Championship.

Unfortunately, the World Chili Championship is annually staged in Terlingua, Texas. Founders claim the event was staged at about the same time Lyndon Johnson was declaring war on poverty. Terlingua was the first community to surrender, these historians claim. Former Seattle International Raceways owner Bill Doner, one of the founders of the World Chili Championship, insists that in the early years the contest received second billing to the submarine races in Dirty Woman Creek.

It's a far piece from Lake Union to Dirty Woman Creek. But on a clear day you can get a whiff of garlic, onions and jalapenos 15 miles away from either location.

GASWORKS CHILI

1/2 pound bacon
3 fresh chili peppers, minced, or 4 dried ones
2 ribs celery, chopped
1 large onion, chopped
4 cloves garlic, minced
3 pounds hamburger
1 can (15 ounces) tomato sauce
1 can (28 ounces) tomatoes, pureed in blender
1 can or jar (8 ounces) jalapeno relish
1 teaspoon salt
1 teaspoon oregano
1 teaspoon cumin
1 teaspoon pepper
3 ounces chili powder
4 cubes chicken bouillon
2 cups water
1 can (28 ounces) red kidney beans or more, if
you want the chili to stretch.

Line a large pot with bacon, cook until crisp, then pour off all but three tablespoons fat. To that remaining fat add the chilis, celery, onion and garlic. Cook until the onion is soft as dawn over Gasworks Park. Add the hamburger and break up with a spoon as it cooks. When the meat is browned add the tomato sauce, pureed tomatoes, the jalapeno relish, the seasonings and spices.

Dissolve the bouillon cubes in the two cups of water and add to the pot. Simmer two or three hours, stirring occasionally. Add the beans plus the cooked and crumbled bacon. Reheat and serve.

That might not win the World Chili Championship but it took first prize in my kitchen when matched against Alice the Artist's bowl of graham crackers and milk.

COMSTOCK CHILI

1 cup dry pinto beans
2 pounds hamburger
1/4 cup cooking oil
1 cup minced onion
1 tablespoon minced garlic
1 large green pepper, chopped
1/2 teaspoon basil
1 teaspoon oregano
3 tablespoons chili powder
1 teaspoon ground cumin
1/4 teaspoon cayenne pepper
1/2 teaspoon black pepper
2 dry chili pepper pods
3 tablespoons flour
1 1/2 quarts chicken stock
2 teaspoons sugar
1/4 cup cracker crumbs
salt to taste

First you have to soak the beans overnight and then cook them in salted water until tender.

Get out your chili pot and glunk in the cooking oil. Crumble in the hamburger and cook, stirring occasionally, until no longer red. Pour or spoon off all grease and then toss into the pot the onion, garlic, green pepper, basil, oregano, chili powder, cumin, cayenne pepper, black pepper and the chili pods.

Stir, cover pot and let all that cook about five minutes. Stir in the flour and when blended pour in the boiling chicken stock. Reduce heat and simmer for an hour. Stir in the sugar and cracker crumbs along with the drained pinto beans. Simmer 10 minutes longer and remove chili pods before serving.

CALAMITY CHILI

2 tablespoons olive oil
3 cloves garlic, minced
1 tablespoon chili powder
1/2 teaspoon dry mustard
1/2 teaspoon ground cumin
1/2 teaspoon celery salt
1/2 teaspoon freshly ground pepper
3/4 pound fresh green beans
1 1/2 cups sliced carrots
1 cup sliced celery
1 onion, chopped
2 green peppers, seeded and chopped
1 can (28 ounces) chopped tomatoes
1 can (32 ounces) chili beans

Heat the oil in a chili pot. Toss in the garlic, chili powder, mustard, cumin, celery salt and black pepper and stir-cook over medium heat 2 minutes.

Add to the pot the juice drained from the tomatoes, the carrots, celery and the green beans, which have been cut into 1-inch pieces, discarding the hard ends. Stir everything around with a genuine Pony Express riding crop, then cover and cook 10 minutes over medium heat.

Add the onion and green pepper, stir, cover and cook another 10 minutes. Finally, add the tomatoes and chili beans, with the bean liquid. Add as much water as you need to achieve the right consistency, about a cup. Cook the chili uncovered until the green beans are cooked. Add salt to taste and this should serve at least six.

I like it spooned into a bowl and topped with grated cheddar cheese and, oh, maybe a little chopped raw onion.

Some sheepherders claim it's even better served over cooked brown rice. But they'd better smile when they say that!

A Rose Bowl

1 can (15 oz.) red kidney beans
1 can (15 oz.) garbanzo beans
1 can (15 oz.) pinto beans
1 medium onion, chopped
1 tablespoon olive oil
3 cloves garlic, minced
1/2 green pepper, chopped
1 can (28 oz.) crushed tomatoes
2 envelopes dry bouillon (beef or chicken)
1 tablespoon Dijon mustard
1 teaspoon dry basil
chili powder (1 to 2 tablespoons)
1 teaspoon oregano
2 teaspoons cumin
1 teaspoon pepper
2 cups frozen corn kernels
2 cups diced zucchini

This represents an alternate view of those who actually like zucchini in their chili.

Drain the liquid off the beans and reserve one cup. Saute the onion, garlic and green pepper in the oil. When they have softened a bit, dump this muck into a pot and add all the other ingredients, including the beans and bean liquid. Simmer until the zucchini is tender. Add cayenne to taste if you want it a bit hotter. Serve sprinkled with Parmesan cheese with a tossed salad and fresh bread.

Redmond Red Chili

2 pounds ground beef
1 large onion, chopped
1 large green pepper, chopped
1-pound can stewed tomatoes
1-pound can tomato sauce
small can tomato paste
1 cup water
1 teaspoon garlic powder
4 tablespoons cumin
5 tablespoons chili powder
salt and pepper to taste
two jalapeno peppers, diced (optional)
large can pinto beans

Brown the meat over high heat, adding the onion and green pepper. Drain off the grease. Add the stewed tomatoes, tomato sauce, tomato paste, water, cumin, chili powder, garlic powder, salt, pepper and the jalapenos.

Bring to a boil, stirring occasionally, lower heat and simmer 15 minutes. Add the pinto beans, simmer another 10 minutes and serve.

Terlingua Mole

2 tablespoons olive oil
4 cloves garlic, minced
2 tablespoons flour
12 cups chicken stock
3 cups tomatoes, diced and drained
6 green onions, including green tops (chopped)
1/4 teaspoon cayenne pepper
1 teaspoon unsweetened cocoa powder
1/2 teaspoon oregano
1/2 teaspoon ground cumin
2 whole chicken breasts, skinned and sliced

Saute the garlic in the oil for two minutes. Add flour and stir-cook two minutes. Add stock in a slow stream, until the flour mixture has been absorbed, and add the rest of the broth. Add all the other ingredients except the chicken, bring to a boil, reduce heat to low and simmer for 90 minutes. Add the chicken (and some chopped fresh cilantro, if you like the herb) and simmer another 20 minutes, or till the chicken is done.

North Bend Beans

2 cups dry pinto beans
water
1 cup diced bacon ends
2 tablespoons chopped onion
1 jalapeno chili chopped
1 fresh tomato, chopped
1 tablespoon salt or to taste
1/4 teaspoon pepper
1/2 teaspoon garlic powder
1 tablespoon chili powder

Wash the beans and soak them overnight. Drain and, in fresh water to cover, cook beans until done. Partially fry the bacon in a skillet, saute the onions, pepper and tomato in bacon grease. Add all to the beans along with the chopped jalapeno and seasonings and simmer at least 15 minutes.

ALKI BEACH IN WEST SEATTLE

CASSEROLES, LUNCH & BRUNCH

ALKI BEACH IN WEST SEATTLE

The settling of Seattle was all the result of an enormous blunder. An advance scout smelled the cocoa butter, heard the engines revving and probably thought he was leading the Arthur Denny Party to Pismo Beach back in 1851.

So the steamer from Portland landed on a rainy November afternoon and of course by that time none of the Indian maidens were sun-bathing any more. There was hardly even a Chevy or Model A cruising the strip, and they were pretty sure they'd made a mistake.

"OK, OK, it's not Pismo Beach," Denny finally admitted to some of the wives who were standing in the rain doing a lot of moaning and sniveling. "But if I can pull off the old $24-and-a-handful-of-beads trick with the treasurer of the Chinook tribe, this place will be another Manhattan in eight or 10 years."

Since Alki is the Chinook word for "by and by" that's what they named their new home, "New York Alki."

These days, of course, nobody wants to be identified with New York, and almost everybody with any sense wants to live in Seattle. So the West Seattle waterfront strip is simply called Alki Beach, and all of the Denny descendants can be located any Saturday night on the beach drive, alternately testing their brakes and engines between 9 p.m. and 3 a.m., unless they happen to be standing in line at Spud's for some fish and chips. Sunday they go to the Alki Homestead restaurant for old-style fried chicken dinners.

Alki Beach is also the religious center for Seattle's sun worshippers, a decidedly curious cult. As the Denny wives found out, cloudless days here are about as common as kangaroos on King Street. Yet merchandisers claim that Seattle leads the nation in the per-capita consumption of sunglasses and suntan oil.

Apparently the residents rush out at the first glimmer of April and buy some Foster Grants. By the time the sun shines again in late August, we've all forgotten that our sunglasses are sitting in a cardboard box, under a large sack of Kitty Litter. So we rush out and buy another pair, along with 10 pounds of cocoa butter.

Rainy days actually provide the most excitement along Alki Beach because you can watch the houses fall off Bonair bluff in a shower of mud. On the rare occasions when the sun shines you are reduced to bicycling, bottom-fishing, bikini-watching or bumper-banging along Beach Drive. Reminds you a lot of Pismo Beach.

Both Spud's and the Alki Homestead Restaurant were closed the week the Denny Party landed so the women opened a few cans, gathered up some mushrooms and eggs and whipped up a few casseroles and such. They also moaned and sniveled a lot.

LANDER AVENUE LOAF

1 pound ham
1 pound ground pork
1 cup bread crumbs
2 eggs
1 cup sour cream
juice of one lemon
juice of one onion
1 teaspoon curry powder
1 teaspoon ginger
1 teaspoon dry mustard
1/4 teaspoon nutmeg
1/4 teaspoon paprika

Mince the ham in a food processor or food grinder and reserve. Do the same with the onion and then pour the resultant mess through a strainer to get the onion juice.

Mix all the ingredients thoroughly by hand, then form into a rounded loaf. Plunk into a lipped oven dish slightly larger than the loaf and shove into a 350° oven for an hour. The last half hour baste generously a few times with the following mixture:

1/4 cup water
1/2 cup cider vinegar
juice of a half lemon
1/2 cup brown sugar
1 teaspoon dry mustard

Simmer the sludge for 10 minutes, and you're ready to baste. When the loaf is cooked let it sit five or 10 minutes to firm up before you carve it with a genuine Chinook tomahawk.

DINNER FOR THE DENNYS

8 ounces noodles, cooked
2 cans tuna, drained
1 1/2 cups sour cream
3/4 cup milk
1 can sliced mushrooms
1 1/2 teaspoons salt
1/4 teaspoon pepper
1/4 cup grated Parmesan cheese
2 tablespoons butter
1/4 cup bread crumbs

Mix the salt and pepper with the milk, then moosh together first eight ingredients and dump into a buttered casserole.

Dribble two tablespoons of melted butter over 1/4 cup of bread crumbs, scatter over the top of the casserole and bake in a 350° oven until bubbly.

A DUWAMISH DINNER

1 can cream of chicken soup
1/2 cup milk
1 1/2 cups shredded cheddar cheese
12-ounce roll of good grade pork sausage
1/4 pound dry noodles, cooked
3 tablespoons chopped green pepper
buttered cracker crumbs

Butter a casserole. Combine the soup and milk in saucepan while heating and mixing it into a satisfactory gloop. Add a cup of the cheese and stir until melted.

While this is happening, you were supposed to be cooking the crumbled sausage in a small skillet.

When done drain off grease and plunk the sausage in the sauce. Add the cooked noodles and green pepper. When heated through and mixed, dump it into the casserole. Top with the cracker crumbs and the last half cup of cheese. Cook, covered, in a 350° oven for 20 minutes. Remove cover, bake another 15 minutes and serve, to four slightly sodden pioneers.

EMMA SCHMITZ QUICHE

1 baked, 10-inch pie shell
4 tablespoons butter
2 tablespoons minced green onion
1 pound thinly sliced fresh mushrooms
1 1/2 teaspoon salt
1 teaspoon lemon juice
4 eggs
1 cup heavy cream
1/8 teaspoon pepper
1/8 teaspoon nutmeg
1/2 cup Swiss cheese, grated

Melt three tablespoons of the butter in a skillet. Add the onions, mushrooms, one teaspoon of salt and the lemon juice. Moosh around with a wooden spoon then cover and simmer over low heat 10 minutes. Uncover, increase heat and stir-cook until the liquid has boiled away.

Plunk the mushroom mixture into the pie shell. Beat together the eggs, cream, the nutmeg, pepper and remaining 1/2 teaspoon of salt. Pour over the mushrooms and scatter the cheese over the top.

Shove the quiche into a preheated, 350° oven for 35 minutes, and then let it sit and relax for a few minutes before carving it up.

Rainy Day Fire Starter

12-ounce roll of hot sausage
1 small onion
3 cups grated raw potatoes
2 eggs
2/3 cup flour
2/3 cup milk
1/8 teaspoon pepper
1 teaspoon baking powder
1 teaspoons salt

After you grate the potatoes, dump them into a bowl with the milk immediately. Peel and grate the onion and stir this into the glunk, too.

In a skillet cook the sausage over medium heat until browned. Pour off the grease. Mix together in a bowl the eggs, flour, milk, pepper, baking powder and salt. When combined add this to the sausage along with the potato mixture. Saute in the pan until browned.

Eggs for a Landing Party

1 1/2 dozen eggs
2 cups white sauce (or 1 can)
8 ounces cream cheese
salt, pepper and chives to taste

Mix everything together, start revolving the ingredients in a large skillet with a wooden spoon or an oar from the dinghy as you slowly cook the eggs. They'll keep a long time in a chafing dish if your guests first have to finish three cups of coffee and a ritualistic tribal dance.

First Family Breakfast

2 tablespoons butter
1 tablespoon oil
1 onion, chopped
1/2 cup ham, chopped
1 can cheese soup
8 beaten eggs
cayenne pepper to taste

What you do is to heat the butter and oil in a skillet, toss in the onion and cook until soft. Then stir in the ham.

In another bowl beat the eggs and stir in the soup (undiluted) and cayenne.

Plunk the ham and onions in the bottom of an oven dish, top with the egg mixture, cover and bake in a 350° oven for 15 minutes, or until it looks more like an omelet than a bowl of graham crackers and milk.

Lighthouse Eggs

6 to 8 flour tortillas
1/2 pound hot pepper cheese
6 eggs
1/2 pound bulk pork sausage

Remove the tortillas from the package, wrap in a damp cloth and place in a warm oven while you cook the filling.

Grate the cheese and beat the eggs.

Brown the sausage in a skillet, breaking up with a wooden spoon as it cooks. Pour off the grease. Into the pan add the eggs and grated cheese and cook as you would scrambled eggs.

Remove pan from heat the instant eggs are done to your liking. Gloop some egg-sausage mixture onto one edge of the tortilla, roll it up and eat as fist food.

Each person will be able to eat a couple of filled tortillas.

Fauntleroy Frittata

1 cup sliced fresh mushrooms
1/3 cup chopped green pepper
1 large clove garlic, minced
2 tablespoons cooking oil
1/2 teaspoon salt
1 1/2 cups soft bread cubes
1/3 cup chopped onion
1 cup chopped zucchini
1/3 cup half and half
5 eggs
1/4 teaspoon pepper
1 cup shredded cheddar cheese
8 ounces cream cheese

Put the cream cheese into the freezer briefly, so it will be easier to cut into half-inch cubes. (The Denny women claimed the whole crummy peninsula was a freezer.)

Heat the oil in a skillet and saute the mushrooms, onions, green pepper, zucchini and garlic until the onions begin to soften.

Beat the eggs with the half and half, salt and pepper. Add the cream cheese cubes, stirring lightly.

Moosh together the mushroom mixture, bread cubes and cheddar cheese. Add the egg-cream cheese glunk and mix lightly so all the ingredients are evenly distributed.

Gloop everything into a greased, 9-inch glass pie plate and bake in a 350° oven for about 45 minutes, or until top is brown and center is set.

Let cool for five to 10 minutes to make it easier to slice, into four large servings or six small ones.

CASCADE CASSEROLE

4 packages frozen chopped spinach
2 pounds ground round
2 medium onions, chopped
3/4 pound fresh mushrooms, sliced
2 teaspoons oregano
1/4 teaspoon garlic powder
salt
2 (10-ounce) cans cream of celery soup
1 (16-ounce) carton sour cream
1 cup uncooked instant rice
Monterey jack cheese

Thaw the spinach and then squeeze it dry in your fists. In a large skillet brown the ground round and chopped onion. Pour off the grease, then stir in the mushrooms, oregano, garlic powder and salt to taste.

Spread the meat mixture over the bottom of an 11-by-16 oven dish. Top with an even layer of spinach.

In a bowl moosh together the undiluted soup, sour cream and the rice. Spread this over the spinach. Top the casserole with slices of cheese and shove into a 350° oven for 20 minutes, or until the rice is cooked and the ingredients are bubbling.

For a little added spice to the dish add a half teaspoon of Tabasco sauce to the soup gloop. And if you want to freeze this dish for a couple of days, don't add the cheese slices until you're ready to put the dish into the oven. Serves six or more.

SALMON QUICHE

1/4 cup sliced mushrooms
1/4 cup minced green onions
1/4 cup chopped fresh tomato
1/4 cup chopped green pepper
1/4 pound cream cheese
4 eggs
1 cup milk
1/2 teaspoon salt
1 teaspoon pepper
nutmeg to taste
1/4 pound smoked salmon
1 uncooked pie shell

Coach says to saute the first four ingredients in a buttered skillet. Cream the cheese and mix in the eggs one at a time. Add the milk and seasonings to the egg gloop.

In the uncooked pie shell place strips of salmon and the sauteed vegetables. Slop the egg mixture over the top. Shove the pie dish into a 350° oven for 15 minutes. Reduce heat to 300° and bake for 45 minutes longer.

BIONDI BRUNCH CASSEROLE

1/2 cup ham, chopped
1/2 pound swiss cheese, shredded
10 eggs
1/2 teaspoon Worcestershire sauce
1/2 teaspoon dry mustard
1 cup half and half

Butter the bottom of a 9-by-13-inch glass dish. Place the ham and cheese in the casserole. Slightly beat the eggs, then add mustard, Worcestershire plus the half and half. Pour the mixture over the ham and cheese.

Bake in a 350° oven for 35 minutes or until the egg mixture is set and golden brown on top. That will serve six to eight.

HEN FRUIT AND HAM

1 cup ham, diced
1/4 cup chopped green onions
6 tablespoons butter or margarine
12 eggs, beaten
14-ounce can sliced mushrooms, drained
cheese sauce (recipe follows)
2 cups fresh bread crumbs
paprika

Melt three tablespoons butter in a skillet and saute the ham and green onion. Add the eggs and stir-cook just until done. Don't overcook. Stir in the drained mushrooms and the cheese sauce. (Recipe below.) Spoon skillet contents into greased 12-by-9-inch oven pan or dish.

Melt the remaining three tablespoons of butter and mix with the bread crumbs. Spread over the egg mixture, sprinkle with paprika, cover and chill overnight.

In the morning bake, uncovered, in a preheated 350° oven for 30 minutes. This will serve six to eight with the coffee cake.

CHEESE SAUCE

2 tablespoons margarine
2 1/2 tablespoons flour
2 cups milk
1/2 teaspoon salt
1/8 teaspoon pepper
1 cup shredded American cheese

Melt margarine in a saucepan over low heat, stir in the flour and cook a minute. Add the milk in blurps. Cook, stirring, until it thickens. Add salt, pepper and cheese. When the cheese melts, the sauce is done.

GRITS FOR BRUNCH

1 cup quick-cooking grits
4 cups water
1 teaspoon salt
1/4 cup margarine, softened
9 ounces processed jalapeno cheese
1 teaspoon Worcestershire sauce
1/8 teaspoon garlic powder
paprika

Add the salt to the water in a saucepan and bring to a boil. Slowly stir in the grits, reduce heat, cover and simmer for 4 1/2 minutes, stirring twice.

Add to the grits the softened margarine, Worcestershire sauce, garlic powder and the cheese, cut into small cubes. (I used a Hoffman brand jalapeno cheese.)

When the cheese has melted, moosh this mess into an oven dish, sprinkle with paprika and shove into that same 400° oven for 20 to 30 minutes.

CABRINI CASSEROLE

1 tablespoon olive oil
2 cans tuna
1 can (8 ounces) mushrooms
1 clove garlic
1 bay leaf
1 teaspoon anchovy paste (optional)
1 teaspoon salt
1/2 teaspoon dry basil
1 teaspoon Tabasco sauce
1 large can (16 ounces) tomato sauce
8 ounces noodles or spaghetti
2 packages (10 ounces each) chopped frozen spinach
1/2 cup grated Parmesan cheese

Cook and squeeze-dry the spinach. Cook the noodles in salted boiling water and drain.

OK, heat the oil in a large skillet. Drain the mushrooms, saving the liquid. Dump the mushrooms and chopped garlic into the pan and saute five minutes. Add the bay leaf, anchovy paste, basil, salt and tomato sauce and simmer 10 minutes. Remove the bay leaf and add to the pan the tuna (I use albacore) and the Tabasco. Cook another five minutes.

Place half the cooked noodles in a casserole. Top with half the spinach and half the sauce. Repeat layers and top with Parmesan cheese.

Heat the casserole in a 350° oven for 30 minutes, or until bubbling hot.

A.M. ENCHILADAS

4 chicken breasts
8 ounces cream cheese
1 cup sour cream
1 can (4 ounces) diced green chilies
1 diced onion
cayenne to taste
salt to taste
Tabasco to taste
flour tortillas (8 to 12)
1 pound grated mozzarella cheese
1/2 cup whipping cream

Bake or broil the chicken just until no longer red in the middle. Sauce the onion in butter until it softens.

OK, shred the chicken meat and mix in a bowl with the cream cheese, sour cream, chilies, onion, cayenne, pepper, salt and Tabasco. Warm the flour tortillas on low heat in an ungreased frying pan. It makes 'em easier to roll.

Fill the tortillas with the chicken mixture, roll and place in a 9-by-13-inch pan. Cover with grated cheese and pour whipping cream evenly over tortillas.

Bake in a 350° oven for 30 minutes or until cheese is bubbly. Serves four to six, and pass the salsa of your choice.

BALLARD BRUNCH

2 cups ham chunks
6 ounces medium egg noodles
1 can cheese soup
14-ounce can chopped green chilies
dash of cayenne pepper
4 green onions, chopped
1/3 cup dried bread crumbs
Butter
Paprika

Cook the noodles in salted water, according to instructions on the package. If you don't, it means you are subconsciously struggling against authority.

Heat the cheese soup and add just enough water to make a sauce. Mix in the chilies, cayenne pepper and green onions.

Put a layer of the drained noodles in a lightly greased casserole. Add half the sauce, some ham chunks, the rest of the noodles, ham chunks and sauce, in that order. Top with dried bread crumbs. Dot with butter, scatter paprika liberally over the top and shove the casserole into a 350° oven for 30 minutes.

ARBORETUM

VEGETABLES

ARBORETUM

There is an annual plant sale as well as a bulb bacchanalia.

"Mushroom, the Irresistible Fungi," was the title of one of the scheduled lectures and another posed the perplexing question, "When is an apple not an apple?"

There are weekly explorer walks. There is usually an enthusiastic turnout for Fourth Thursday Weeders Day. It's a great place for a picnic, if you don't get trampled by the occasional Volksmarcher headed for Foster Island.

Certainly you would never suspect that the University of Washington Arboretum would have been an object of seething controversy and protest over the years.

Don't you know about the Ban the Evergreen Bridge rallies which once shook our community? Have you forgotten that 275 Arboretum habitues once petitioned to have the duck lagoon declared a nude beach? Is your sense of history so incomplete you're ignorant of the countless skirmishes and holding actions fought on behalf of the Arboretum by Dr. Hugo Winkenwerden, dean of the UW Forestry Department during the emerging years?

The, err, roots of the Arboretum extend back to 1924 when a group of Seattle gardening enthusiasts convinced Seattle park commissioners that our climate and soil could support 98 percent of the plant materials of the world, not to mention a few skinny-dippers. Ten years later the UW agreed to co-sponsor the project at Washington Park, which was eventually completed as a federal work relief project during the Great Depression.

Master plans for the 200-acre park adjoining Lake Washington were drawn up by the Olmsted Brothers of Massachusetts. It was their father who laid out Central Park in New York. In their Montlake version, the Olmsted Brothers decided to leave out the muggers.

Eleanor Roosevelt once traveled to Seattle to plant a tree in the Arboretum, right next to the George Washington Elm. Originally a slip from the tree under which George Washington took command of the Continental Army, the G.W. Elm was donated by the Daughters of the American Revolution, and it should not be confused with the Japanese Maples, which were planted shortly before Pearl Harbor.

Today, if you mind yourself and keep your clothes on, you can roam along Rhododendron Glen and Winter Garden, across Foster Island and along Azalea Way to the Japanese Garden.

Or you can rent a canoe at the nearby University of Washington boat house and cruise past the fishermen, darting swallows and pastures of water lilies to examine the Arboretum from the water side.

On autumn football Saturdays some of the most lavish pre-game picnics in the history of intercollegiate athletics are served at the Arboretum to the fans headed for Husky Stadium. On warm spring afternoons families and lovers stroll down through pink and green corridors of flowering plum and crabapple trees.

Visitors are not allowed to probe, pester or pick the plants but afterward they can rush home and open a can of something green.

ARBORETUM BEANS

fresh, frozen or canned green beans to serve four
1 large onion
1/2 teaspoon rosemary
1/2 teaspoon marjoram
1/2 teaspoon salt
1/4 cup sunflower seeds
4 tablespoons butter

Cook beans until tender (or reheat). Peel and coarsely chop the onion and scatter over the top of the beans in a pot. Add the herbs, salt and seeds, mix and let simmer over medium-low heat for a few minutes. Add the butter in four splats and when it has melted mix the beans lightly and serve.

GARLIC GREENERY

1 bunch broccoli
olive oil
2 minced cloves garlic
Italian seasonings
salt, pepper

Separate broccoli into flowerettes. Peel and thinly slice the large stalks. Toss the stalks into simmering salted water for one minute. Add the flowerettes and simmer everything another 2 1/2 minutes. Drain.

Toss the drained broccoli into a skillet containing a covering of olive oil and the garlic. Sprinkle with Italian seasonings to your taste, add salt and pepper and stir-fry briefly until hot but still crisp.

POPEYE'S PEPPERS

4 green peppers
4 beaten eggs
1/2 cup grated Parmesan cheese
1/2 cup bread crumbs
1 cup sour cream
1 package frozen, chopped spinach
pinch of oregano
pinch of garlic powder
salt, pepper to taste
1/2 cup olive oil

Cut tops off the peppers and remove seeds and white pith. Don't give me that funny look. Get the pith out of there!

The spinach should be thawed and then squeezed dry in your hands. Mix it with the eggs, cheese, crumbs, sour cream and seasonings. Fill the four peppers, plop in a shallow baking pan, drizzle oil over the peppers and bake an hour in a 375° oven.

CAULIFLOWER CASSEROLE

1 cup elbow macaroni
3 tablespoons butter
3 tablespoons flour
1 1/2 teaspoon salt
1/2 teaspoon paprika
1 1/2 cups milk
1 cup shredded cheddar cheese
1 1/2 cup steamed and chopped cauliflower
a sprinkling of cayenne pepper
1/4 cup buttered bread crumbs

OK, cook the macaroni in salted, boiling water for 10 minutes. Drain and rinse. Melt the butter in a saucepan and stir in the flour, salt, paprika and cayenne to taste. Gradually add the milk, stirring until thickened.

Adds the cheese and the steamed cauliflower. Fold in the cooked macaroni. Pour into a greased casserole and sprinkle with bread crumbs. Bake 15 minutes in a 350° oven, and this will serve four.

SPINACH CASSEROLE FOR A CROWD

5 packages frozen, chopped spinach
1 cup butter
1 large onion, chopped
2 cloves garlic, minced
1 cup cream
1 cup milk
1/2 cup dry bread crumbs
1 teaspoon marjoram
1 teaspoon salt
1/4 teaspoon pepper
1/2 cup grated Parmesan cheese

Thaw the spinach and lightly squeeze out excess liquid.

Melt the butter in a large pot, dump in the onion and garlic, let it jump around and sputter indignantly until soft and then dump in all the other ingredients except for a quarter cup of Parmesan.

Moosh everything around, then plop into a greased casserole and sprinkle top with the reserved cheese. Shove into a 350° oven for 30 minutes or until top is browned. Serves 10 to 12.

ALL-STAR SQUASH

1 medium acorn squash
3 tablespoons soft butter
1 tablespoon brown sugar
1/4 teaspoon cinnamon
1/4 teaspoon salt
pinch of nutmeg
1 teaspoon grated orange peel
juice of one-half orange
1/4 cup chopped pecans

Whack the squash in half lengthwise and discard the seeds. Moosh together the butter, sugar, salt, spices, orange peel and juice. Stir in the nuts.

Pour water a half-inch deep in an oven dish. Plunk in the two squash halves, cut side up, and fill with the butter-sugar gloop. Cover the oven dish with foil and cook in a 375° oven for 40 minutes. Uncover and bake a final 30 minutes or until done.

Obviously, this serves two.

GREEK GREEN BEANS

1 pound fresh green beans
1 onion, sliced
1/2 cup olive oil, or to taste
2 tomatoes, peeled and chopped
1/4 cup chopped parsley
1/2 teaspoon dried oregano
1 teaspoon salt
pepper

Wash, destring beans and cut in half. Heat oil in a saucepan and saute the onions. Add tomatoes, beans, parsley, oregano, pepper and one cup water. Simmer an hour, add salt and let sit a couple of minutes before serving. I like it hot. The Greeks eat it cold, or at room temperature.

SESAME SPINACH

1 pound fresh spinach
3 tablespoons black sesame seeds
2 tablespoons soy sauce
1 tablespoon sugar
dash of MSG

Wash the spinach in an authentic Huron foot bath, then parboil two minutes in lightly salted water. Drain and dump the spinach in cold water immediately, if you want it to remain bright green.

Squeeze out the water, form the spinach into strands and cut into 1 1/2-inch hunks.

Grind the sesame seeds in a mortar. Add the soy, sugar and MSG and mix with the spinach. As a side dish this serves four, at room temperature.

SINFUL GRASS

8 ounces spaghetti
6 tablespoons butter
10 asparagus spears
2 large eggs
3/4 cup heavy cream
3 tablespoons freshly grated Parmesan cheese
1/4 teaspoon grated nutmeg
juice of one lemon
3 tablespoons minced parsley

Cook the spaghetti in boiling salted water until barely tender.

While it is cooking, melt the butter in a pan. Add the asparagus, cut into 1-inch lengths and cook over low heat about five minutes.

Break the eggs into a bowl and add the cream, cheese, nutmeg, parsley and half the lemon juice. With an authentic Roman fly whisk, whip everything around until blended into a sauce.

Drain the cooked pasta in a colander. Return it to the warm pan along with the asparagus, butter and lemon sauce. Toss the asparagus around in the sauce over low heat for about 30 seconds. Taste and add more lemon juice if you think it needs it. This will serve two to three as a main dish, or more as a first course.

SINLESS GRASS

2 tablespoons canola oil
10 spears asparagus cut in 1-inch lengths
1 clove garlic, minced
3 tablespoons fresh grated ginger root
4 green onions, chopped
half of a green pepper, diced
1 pound sea scallops
1/2 pound fresh mushrooms, sliced
1 tablespoon dry sherry
3 tablespoons sesame seeds, toasted

Heat a skillet, add the oil and stir-fry the asparagus pieces for two minutes, then remove. Add to the pan the garlic, ginger, green onions and green pepper. Saute 30 seconds, then add the scallops and mushrooms, and cook until scallops are white in the center. (If you use large scallops, cut them in half.) Add the asparagus, sherry and sesame seeds, and when everything is hot, serve up on four plates. You can scatter fresh minced cilantro over the top if you like.

WATERFRONT TROLLEY

POTATOES, RICE, ETC.

THE WATERFRONT TROLLEY

Who says we don't have any more empire builders in the vast Northwest?

Certainly you have overlooked George Benson. In his shadow such railway barons as J.I. Blair and J.P. Morgan shrivel into insignificance.

Considers the achievements of George Benson. He not only conceived and directed construction of The Great P and P Railway, he painted the cars, hammered in the final spike on the track and then lifted up his trombone and played a musical salute at the dedication.

The Great P and P runs (obviously) between Pioneer Square and Pier 70, along the waterfront with much tooting of whistle and clanging of bell.

People laughed when City Councilman Benson first suggested hauling two or three 1927-vintage trolley cars here from Melbourne, Australia, to run on the Burlington tracks. Yet that first summer The Great P and P was the most profitable route in the Metro system. In four months, fares on The Great P and P surpassed projections, which had been drawn up for a full year.

True, it's not the Orient Express. The Orient Express wasn't built out of Tasmanian mahogany; it doesn't have a circular foot pedal operating the bell, and it doesn't toot-toot past a half-dozen fish and chips counters in only 1.6 miles.

J.I. Blair and J.P. Morgan were motivated by money. George Benson was motivated by his fascination with trains, going back to his childhood. He also likes to play the trombone and does so still with the Husky Alumni Band.

While the bureaucrats were still arguing about the financial feasibility of The Great P and P, George was involved in trolley-painting parties with civic leaders like Bruce Nordstrom, who probably doesn't do a thing around his house.

If they ever engrave a silver plaque and mount it at one of the seven terminals of The Great P and P, George Benson's name should be at the top, over those of Sir Rupert Hamer and Wayne E. Mayhle.

Sir Rupert was the dignitary representing Australia at the official trolley dedication.

As for Wayne E. Mayhle, he was driving his car across a waterfront track the first full day The Great P and P was in operation. His engine stalled halfway through the intersection and Wayne E. Mayhle was broadsided by a few thousand pounds of Tasmanian mahogany.

Don't blame George Benson. He was probably home practicing his trombone while his wife cooked up one of the following recipes.

P AND P POTATOES

4 pounds potatoes
1/2 cup cream
1/4 cup grated onion
1 teaspoon salt
1 stick softened butter
2 egg yolks
pepper to taste
4 egg whites
5 thin slices of onion

Peel and cook the potatoes in boiling water until you can spear one with a fork without drawing blood. Dump into the large bowl of your mixer along with the cream, grated onion and salt. Beat and when just about smooth add the stick of butter, the egg yolks, the pepper and more salt if you think it needs some.

In another bowl beat the four egg whites with a pinch of salt and a pinch of cream of tartar until it forms peaks. Fold this glunk into the potatoes in a souffle dish or casserole. Top with the onion slices, brush with butter and bake in a 325° oven for 45 minutes.

PHINNEY POTATOES

2 medium potatoes
1/2 cup grated Swiss cheese
2 tablespoons minced onion
1 teaspoon chopped parsley
salt, pepper
butter
paprika

Heat oven to 350° while you are peeling and coarsely grating potatoes into a small bowl of cold water. Drain and shake hands with the potatoes, until they are fairly dry. Combine with the cheese, onion, parsley and salt and pepper to taste.

Generously coat the inside of two custard cups with butter and sprinkle with paprika. Divide the potato mixture between cups, pressing down firmly.

Bake uncovered in center rack of oven for 40 minutes or until edges are brown and crisp and the center no longer has the texture of Irish mush.

Loosen the potatoes around the edges with a knife and dump upside down on two plates because that's how many it will serve.

RAILROAD AVENUE SPUDS

8 medium potatoes
1 pint sour cream
1 1/2 cups grated cheddar cheese
6 green onions, tops and all, chopped
1 1/2 teaspoons salt
pepper
paprika

Boil the unpeeled potatoes until just tender, peel and then shred. Plunk in a casserole and add the sour cream, green onion, one cup of the cheese and the salt and pepper. Cover and refrigerate overnight.

Forty minutes before dinner sprinkle with paprika and shove the uncovered casserole into a 350° oven. Fifteen minutes before it is done sprinkle with the last half cup of cheese and return to the oven.

TROLLEY TATERS

1 1/2 pounds new potatoes
5 tablespoons butter
1/3 cup chopped green onions
3 tablespoons flour
1 1/2 cups chicken broth
1 teaspoon caraway seed
1/2 teaspoon ground cumin
salt, pepper
1 cup shredded Swiss cheese
1/2 cup coarse fresh bread crumbs
1/8 teaspoon paprika

Boil the potatoes until just tender, cool and peel. Cut the potatoes into half-inch cubes and plunk in a shallow casserole.

Melt the butter in a pan, then set aside two tablespoons. Add the onions to remaining butter and saute until tender. Add the flour and stir-cook two minutes. Stir in the chicken broth and when smooth add the caraway, cumin and salt and pepper to taste.

Pour this sauce over the potatoes, top with the Swiss cheese. Toss the bread crumbs with the remaining two tablespoons of butter, sprinkle over the cheese and sprinkle again with paprika.

Bake uncovered for 25 minutes in a 400° oven. If you refrigerate it first, you should heat it for 35 minutes. It will serve four to six.

Mashed Potato Ring

6 cups potatoes mashed without butter or milk
1 cup grated sharp cheddar cheese
butter

Season the potatoes well with salt, pepper and paprika. Fold cheese into the spuds and spoon into a heavily buttered ring mold. Brush with a tablespoon of butter and shove into the oven (at 325°) for 30 minutes.

Unmold the potato ring on an oven-proof platter. Brush the top with more butter and then shove under the oven broiler until crisp and brown, about four minutes.

Fill the ring with carrot sticks which have been steamed until tender in butter and a teaspoonful of sugar mixed with just enough water to cover the bottom of the pan.

Swiss Scalloped Spuds

2 cups half and half
1 large clove garlic, minced
3/4 cup freshly grated Parmesan cheese
1/2 cup grated Swiss cheese
2 1/2 pounds baking potatoes
freshly ground nutmeg to taste
1/4 teaspoon white pepper

Pour the half and half into a saucepan. Add the garlic, one-half cup Parmesan and one-quarter cup of Swiss cheese. Cook over medium heat just until the cheese begins to melt. Do not boil.

Peel and thinly slice the spuds. Sprinkle with nutmeg, white pepper and salt to taste. Layer the potatoes in a well-buttered 14-inch oven dish. Glunk the milk-cheese mixture over the potatoes. Sprinkle the remaining quarter-cup of Parmesan and quarter-cup of Swiss cheese over the top. Bake on the middle shelf of a 400° oven for an hour.

Posh Polenta

8 cups chicken broth
1 cup white wine
3 cloves garlic, put through a press
4 green onions, minced
1/4 cup minced parsley
2 teaspoons rosemary
3 cups instant polenta
olive oil

You can now find instant polenta in most of the better supermarkets. You only have to stir it about five minutes. It you are going to make authentic polenta, hire one of the Seahawk linebackers to stir it for you, because I think you start stirring on Monday and finish Wednesday night.

OK, put all of the above ingredients except the polenta and olive oil in a pot and bring to a boil. Slowly stir in the polenta. Reduce heat to medium and stir-cook five minutes. Pour the resulting muck onto a cookie sheet, creating a slab about 1/2-inch thick. Let cool, then refrigerate.

When firm cut in squares and brush on both sides with the olive oil. Then you can saute it, broil it or singe it over a barbecue fire.

This can be served plain or with a marinara spaghetti sauce.

Rice with Sage

2 tablespoons butter or margarine
1 teaspoon powdered sage
1 cup chicken broth
3/4 cup long grain rice
1/4 cup grated Parmesan cheese

Heat the butter in a saucepan and when it's melted add the sage, turn off the heat and let it sit while you:

Heat the broth to boiling, add the rice, lower heat and simmer uncovered until rice is tender, 12 to 14 minutes.

Gloop the rice into a serving dish, toss with the sage butter and Parmesan.

Denny Regrade Rice

1 cup raw rice
1 can drained mushrooms
1/8 teaspoon pepper
1/4 teaspoon nutmeg
2 tablespoons sherry
2 tablespoons butter
1 10-ounce package frozen peas
1/4 teaspoon marjoram
2 cups boiling chicken bouillon

Thaw the peas at room temperature. Combine all the ingredients in a casserole, mix well, cover and shove into a 350° oven for an hour, or until all the liquid has been absorbed.

Fluff with a fork. It serves four.

THE AQUARIUM

CRAB AND SHRIMP

THE AQUARIUM

You'll find inside a salmon run, some seals and otters, too.
Anemones and urchins and a gross of octopoo.
Piranha for your mother-in-law, electric eels for the kids.
Some slimy sea cucumbers and a few man-eating squid.

If the residents of the Seattle Aquarium can survive that little ditty, which was sung by the members of the City Council on the day the complex was opened, then they should be able to stomach even an occasional tainted horse clam.

And they seem to be surviving very nicely, octopoos and all. Our prize-winning aquarium was the first one in the world linked directly with the ocean outside and actually serves as a seagoing motel for departing and arriving silver salmon.

The salmon, however, take second billing to the sea otters and northern fur seal pups. Over the years virtually all the residents of the aquarium have taken second billing to furred creatures with names like Tichuck, Chumaka, Cocotl, Doc and Big Al. The otters execute flips and barrel rolls with their babies clutching frantically, hang-glider fashion, and all the spectators say, "Ohhh" and "Ahhhh" and "Aren't they cute?"

Well, maybe they are, but it seems to me that the sea otters are products of an enormous public-relations hype. The Seattle Aquarium has sponsored "Name the Otter" contests and color crayon competitions. A press release is issued whenever an otter burps. And countless volunteers have been recruited over the years for round-the-clock Otter Watches, presumably to prevent Etika from running down to the Lock Spot Tavern for a beer and a few salted herring at 1 a.m.

Have the Seattle Aquarium people ever recruited any toadfish watchers or sponsored any coloring contests featuring eelpouts or sticklebacks? Not likely. They have not been selected as darlings of the media. Is that fair? Don't you think that octopoos have feelings, too?

Oh, sure, the Seattle Aquarium also features a tide pool, fish ladders and a popular Touching Pool for little tots. It goes heavy on turtles, snails and starfish. Hardly ever do the little people get to touch sharks, lionfish or wolf eels.

It's a great aquarium nevertheless, and you should hustle the kinfolk from Wolf Breath down there quick next time they're in town.

Afterwards you can take them home for a Puget Sound feast. You could serve them some broiled dogfish steaks or maybe a nice squid-sculpin-sea urchin stew. That's the best way I know to get relatives pointed back toward Wolf Breath in a hurry.

If that is not your immediate goal, serve them some of the following:

CRACKED CRAB VERMOUTH

1 stick butter
2 tablespoons cornstarch
1 cup dry vermouth
1 can (14 ounces) chicken broth
2 tablespoons chopped parsley
2 tablespoons minced garlic
1 tablespoon soy sauce
1 tablespoon lemon juice
1 teaspoon sugar
2 Dungeness crabs, cleaned and cracked

In a pot melt the butter. Remove from heat and stir in cornstarch. Add the vermouth and chicken broth, stirring, as you return pot to heat. Add the parsley, garlic, soy, lemon juice and sugar. Bring to a boil, reduce heat, cover and simmer 10 minutes.

Add the crabs, moosh everything around, spooning the sauce over the sections. Cover and simmer until crab is heated through, 10 to 15 minutes.

BRIANWOOD BARBECUED CRAB

2 cups tomato catsup
1 cup water
1 whole clove
1 teaspoon season salt or seafood seasoning
1/2 teaspoon thyme
1/2 teaspoon basil
1/2 teaspoon MSG
1/2 teaspoon sugar
1 tablespoon Worcestershire sauce
1 teaspoon prepared horseradish
1 to 2 crabs

Clean and crack the crab. In a large pot gloop together the catsup, water, spices, Worcestershire and horseradish. When simmering add the crab pieces, reduce heat and let burble for 10 to 15 minutes. Serve up the crab on plates and pass the excess sauce in a gravy boat.

CRAB LEGS LAURELHURST

60 crab legs
1/2 pound butter
1 cup dry white wine
sprig of rosemary
1/4 teaspoon tarragon
pinch of thyme
2 tablespoons parsley, chopped
cracker crumbs

This will serve the six-man board of Seattle First National Bank. (You may need a second mortgage to finance the crab legs.)

Melt the butter in a saucepan with the wine and herbs. Let simmer until reduced by half then set aside to cool slightly. Dip each crab leg into the sauce, roll in fine cracker crumbs, salting and peppering lightly. Arrange on a flat baking dish. Sprinkle a little sauce over the top, then shove under a broiler until golden. Turn, return to oven until sizzling on second side and serve. Pour the rest of the sauce through a sieve, over the legs.

DUNGENESS FRITTERS

1/2 pound crab meat
3 tablespoons chopped green onion
2 tablespoons chopped parsley
2 eggs, slightly beaten
1 teaspoon Worcestershire
1/4 cup unsifted flour
2 teaspoons baking powder
1/8 teaspoon salt
3 tablespoons butter
lemon wedges

Gloop together the crab, onion, parsley, eggs and Worcestershire. Sift together into the crab glunk the flour, baking powder and salt. Stir just until mixed.

Heat the butter in a skillet and fry tablespoonfuls of the crab mixture turning once, until brown on both sides. Serve with lemon wedges and this will make about 16 small fritters.

SEWARD STUFFED CRAB

2 crabs
2 onions, minced
2 cloves garlic, minced
5 tablespoons olive oil
2 chopped tomatoes
2 tablespoons chopped parsley
1 cup dry white wine
2 teaspoons salt
2 teaspoons sugar
pinch of cayenne
1/2 cup dry bread crumbs
butter

Remove the meat from the crab. Fry the onion and garlic slowly in the oil. Increase heat, add the tomatoes and cook until most of liquid evaporates. Add the parsley and wine and cook over a hot fire until wine has evaporated.

Blend the crab butter you have removed from the body shell and mix this into the sauce with the crab meat, salt, sugar and cayenne. Spoon into four ramekins (or four clean crab shells). Sprinkle top with crumbs, dot with butter and brown in a 400° oven.

PAT'S CHUPAY

A dozen or more slices of white bread
1 cube butter, melted
4 cups whole milk
8 eggs (or substitute)
salt, pepper, cayenne
1/2 cup mayonnaise
1 pound small shrimp
1 pound fresh scallops
1/2 pound medium sharp cheddar cheese
4 tablespoons onion flakes
2 cans cream of shrimp soup
1/2 cup grated Parmesan
paprika

Heat two cups of milk to a boiling point. Cut scallops in bite-size pieces and poach in the milk about three minutes. Turn off the heat and add the rest of the milk. Allow the seafood to steep while you cut the bread into 2-inch squares.

Butter a large serving dish or pan. Cover with a single layer of bread squares and drizzle with three tablespoons melted butter. Scatter the shrimp over the bread. Drain the scallops and add them, too. Distribute the onion flakes over the top.

OK, next you spread the thinly sliced cheddar over the fish. Cover with the remaining bread cubes. Pour the remaining butter over the top.

Beat the eggs, or the egg substitute, with the mayonnaise. Add the warm milk. Season this gloop with salt, pepper and cayenne and slop it over the chupay.

You can cover this with foil and refrigerate up to 24 hours. If you do, remove from your refrigerator two hours before you plan to feed 10 to 12 guests.

The final stage of cooking involves pouring the two cans of undiluted shrimp soup over the top and sprinkling with a final layer of Parmesan and paprika.

If the dish is now at room temperature, you can shove it into a 350° oven for 50 to 60 minutes.

DISCOVERY BAY DINNER

1 cup chicken broth
1 cup dry white wine
2 green onions, minced
1/2 teaspoon dried basil
1/2 pound scallops
1/4 pound shrimp
1/4 pound crab meat
4 artichoke hearts, halved
3 tablespoons butter
4 tablespoons flour
1/2 cup milk
1 egg yolk
1/4 cup heavy cream
few drops lemon juice
salt and pepper

1/4 cup grated Parmesan cheese

Bring the chicken broth, wine, green onions and basil to a boil in a saucepan. Dump in the scallops and the shelled and deveined shrimp. Reduce heat, cover and let simmer not more than five minutes.

Remove the scallops and shrimp and boil down the liquid left in the pot until it has been reduced to one cup. Strain it into a bowl.

Dirty up another pan by melting three tablespoons of butter and then, off the heat, stir in the flour. Pour in the reduced broth and half cup of milk and stir-cook with a whisk, bringing to a boil until it is smooth and thick. Lower heat and beat in the egg yolk, then the quarter cup of cream. Simmer for a minute, then add lemon juice, salt and pepper to taste.

Butter four ramekins or individual oven dishes. Drain the scallops and shrimp of any liquid and mix with the crab and artichoke hearts. Divide into the four dishes, pour the sauce over all, top with the grated cheese and shove into a 375° oven for 15 minutes.

DRUGSTORE SHRIMP-CRAB DINNER

1 can crab meat
1 can shrimp
1/2 cup of butter or margarine
1 small onion, chopped
1 1/2 tablespoons flour
1/2 teaspoon dry mustard
1/4 teaspoon paprika
1/4 teaspoon salt
cayenne to taste
1/2 teaspoon Worcestershire
1/2 cup milk
1/4 cup dry sherry
2 tablespoons bread crumbs
Parmesan cheese

Melt a tablespoon and a half of the butter in a saucepan and saute the chopped onion until until soft.

Stir in the flour, mustard, paprika, salt, cayenne to taste and the Worcestershire. Slowly add the milk and reduce heat. Stir until thick and smooth then add the sherry and the drained crab and shrimp.

Fill two or three oven-proof dishes with the mixture.

In a saucepan melt the remaining butter and mix with the crumbs. Scatter this over the top of the crab-shrimp mixture. Then scatter with a layer of grated Parmesan and another sprinkle of paprika. Bake in a 375° oven for 15 to 20 minutes.

THE SALMON FLEET

SALMON AND HALIBUT

THE SALMON FLEET

You say some visitors are headed your way from The Great Flatlands.

Be sure they have the opportunity to take a ride in one of our glass-bottom boats, out over the coral reefs, so they can view the tropical fish.

Well, maybe we don't have bona fide pink and yellow coral in Puget Sound, but we have some nifty rocks and better mud than most.

Sure, sure, I know. You want directions to the nearest glass-bottom boat. The truth of the matter is that we don't have any because we don't need them. You want a good look at the water, you lean over the side of the boat.

In fact that's the way most visitors from The Great Flatlands prefer to travel, when aboard one of the salmon charters out of a seaside resort like Westport.

"Whee! Wow! Some Fun!" they whoop, as the skipper backs the boat out of the moorage slip. But once the Lazy Lucy has crossed the Westport bar, all of the tourists suddenly seem to swallow their tongues. It is then that they begin to examine the wave tops at close range, while hanging over the side of the boat.

Chances are that they took Dramamine tablets with breakfast, as a precaution. But the pill is likely resting inside a two-pound ball of cholesterol from morning fare of bacon, eggs and buttered toast. The six cups of coffee are also a bad idea, although considered a minimal dose for someone attempting to open one eyelid at 4 a.m. in a Westport motel.

Of course you don't have to drive all the way to Westport or Sekiu to get seasick. It's just that the waves, and the salmon, are more numerous near the coast.

A lot of Seattle residents still chase salmon through Puget Sound, near hot spots with names like Possession, Humpy Hollow and Eagle Bluff.

Oh, it isn't like the olden days when you could catch your limit by banging the salmon over the head with a stout oar, minutes from one of the West Seattle or Ballard boat houses.

The first rental outfit in operation here, in the 1880s, was the Budlong Boat House between Columbia and Madison on Seattle's waterfront. It burned down during the Great Fire of '89, along with most of Seattle.

At one time there were a half-dozen boat houses on what is now the Seacrest property near Duwamish Head.

But the boat house with the most famous name was probably Ray's. It was built in the 1930s. They began to serve hamburgers there, as well as frozen herring, in 1946. For the next 25 years a succession of fish and chips operations fed the fishermen. But starting in 1973 Ray's became better known for its haute cuisine than as a launching pad for hooknose hunters.

The present, posh establishment near the entrance to the Ballard Locks replaced the restaurant destroyed by fire in May of 1987. This blaze wasn't as big as The Great Seattle Fire, but it lit up the sky and could be seen 10 miles away.

But firemen reported the appearance of a frantic female who demanded a pass through the fire lines at about 7:45 in the evening. They shrugged and pointed to the blaze when she said she was headed for Ray's Boat House.

"But I have 8 p.m. reservations," she proclaimed.

Finally one of the smoke smudged fire laddies delivered the sad news.

"Lady, I think your supper is burned."

These days the cooking fire isn't quite so hot at Ray's.

But if you are unable to secure an 8 p.m. reservation you might want to treat the visitors from The Great Flatlands with one of these seafood feasts.

BOAT HOUSE BUFFET SALMON

1 whole salmon, about 6 pounds
3/4 cup dry white wine
1/4 teaspoon dried thyme
1/4 teaspoon dried rosemary
1/2 teaspoon dried basil
1/4 teaspoon dried tarragon
handful of celery leaves
3 green onions, minced
3 slices lemon
4 peppercorns
1/2 teaspoon salt

Pour the wine into a non-copper pan, add all the other ingredients except the salmon and lemon and steep for 30 minutes. Strain and reserve the liquid. Preheat oven to 350°.

Rinse the salmon, lay it on a sheet of aluminum foil and spread the lemon slices inside the fish. Pour the liquid inside and over the fish, bring foil up and around and seal securely.

Place on a rimmed baking sheet and bake for 12 to 15 minutes a pound. Serve cold, skinned, with This Sauce smeared over the top or served on the side.

THIS SAUCE

Mix a half-cup of mayonnaise with a half-cup of sour cream. Add a tablespoon of minced shallots, a tablespoon of minced capers, with lemon juice, salt and white pepper to taste.

SEAVIEW SALMON

6 salmon steaks or 2 1/2 pounds fillets
1/3 cup melted butter
1/2 teaspoon salt
1/2 teaspoon paprika
1 teaspoon Worcestershire sauce
1 teaspoon prepared mustard
2 tablespoons soy sauce
2 tablespoons catsup
1 clove garlic, minced

Arrange the steaks in one layer of a greased oven dish or pan. Combine the butter, salt, paprika and Worcestershire. Slop this over the salmon. Bake uncovered in a 350° oven. It will take about 20 minutes for steaks or about 30 minutes for fillets. Remove fish to a warm platter.

Pour pan juices into saucepan. Add the mustard, soy, catsup and garlic. Simmer briskly for a couple of minutes. Serve up the salmon in portions and gloop the sauce over each one. Serves six.

KING STREET SALMON STEAKS

4 salmon steaks
1/4 cup cooking oil
2 tablespoons lemon juice
2 tablespoons soy sauce
1/2 teaspoon dry mustard
1/2 teaspoon ground ginger
1/8 teaspoon garlic powder

Plunk the salmon steaks in a shallow dish. Moosh together the oil, lemon juice, soy, mustard, ginger and garlic powder and pour over the fish. Let it dog paddle in the marinade for about an hour, turning once.

Drain the fish, reserving the marinade. Place steaks on broiler pan and broil three inches from the heat for five minutes. Turn, brush with the marinade and broil another five minutes or until done. Serves four.

SALTCHUCK SALMON CAKES

1 can (15 ounces) salmon
1 cup fresh bread crumbs
1 egg
1/4 cup minced green onion
2 tablespoons lemon juice
1 teaspoon Worcestershire sauce
1/4 teaspoon lemon pepper

Drain and flake the salmon. If you use red salmon the cakes will be really good. If you use less expensive pink salmon they will merely be terrific.

Moosh together with your hands the salmon and all other ingredients. Form into eight patties, plunk them on a spray-oiled cookie sheet and shove into a pre-heated 400° oven for five minutes.

HIGHLANDS HALIBUT CHEEKS

12 halibut cheeks
2 eggs
1/2 cup dry sherry
2 tablespoons minced ginger root
salt, pepper
cracker crumbs

Put an egg into your Gucci and beat it. Or you can use a wire whisk to stir the two eggs into the sherry. Add the ginger root and salt and pepper to taste.

Dip the cheeks into the sherry-egg mixture, then coat in cracker crumbs.

Fry until golden in a mixture of canola oil and butter. This will serve three to four.

HAMLIN HALIBUT

Buy halibut steaks or fillets to serve four. Rub each portion with a mixture of olive oil and Worcestershire sauce. Sprinkle with garlic salt and onion powder. Cook 20 to 25 minutes in a covered barbecue. Or plunk in an oiled dish, cover with foil and cook 20 to 30 minutes in a preheated 350° oven.

Top with this special sauce:

3 tablespoons flour
3 tablespoons butter
1 cup clam nectar
1/2 cup dry white wine
4 ounces mushrooms, sliced
4 ounces small shrimp
lemon juice
salt, pepper

Melt the butter in a saucepan, add the flour and stir-cook a minute or two. Add the clam nectar and wine and stir-cook until smooth. Add the mushrooms and shrimp and cook over low heat 10 minutes, stirring a couple of times. Add salt and lemon juice (two to four tablespoons) to taste.

Divide sauce over fish and holler, "Grub's on!" Serves four.

HERBED HALIBUT

halibut steaks to serve four
1/3 cup butter or margarine
2 tablespoons minced green onion
1 clove garlic, minced
1/2 teaspoon salt
generous grinding of pepper
1/4 teaspoon dried thyme
1/2 teaspoon dried basil
1 tablespoon lemon juice

Line a broiler pan with aluminum foil, replace the top and plunk on the fish.

Meanwhile cream the butter, onion, garlic and herbs together. Gradually beat in the lemon juice. Spread half the herb butter over the fish and broil two inches from the heat for three or four minutes. Carefully turn the fish with a pancake flipper, spread with remaining herb butter and broil a final three to four minutes or just until the center meat flakes with a fork.

Serve steaks on a warm platter with any sauces remaining in the bottom of the broiler pan poured over the top.

TIN-SALMON SUPPER

1 pound can salmon
3 tablespoons butter
3 tablespoons flour
milk
1 quart cooked potatoes, sliced
1/2 cup mayonnaise
1/2 cup grated cheddar cheese
1 teaspoon prepared mustard
1 teaspoon Worcestershire sauce

Pour the liquid from the canned salmon into large measuring cup and add milk until you have two cups of liquid. Flake the salmon in a bowl.

Melt the butter in a pot, stir in the flour and when smooth add the liquid and stir-cook until it thickens.

Plunk into a greased casserole dish the potatoes, salmon and sauce in alternate layers. Combine mayonnaise, cheese, mustard and Worcestershire and slop this mess over the top.

Bake in a 375° oven for 30 minutes.

SEACREST CASSEROLE

2 large potatoes
olive oil
4 halibut or cod steaks
2 tomatoes, halved
4 cloves garlic, minced
1/2 cup minced parsley
4 green onions, minced
1 teaspoon fresh rosemary
1 teaspoon fresh thyme
lemon juice

Peel and thinly slice the potatoes, drop in boiling water for four minutes, then drain and pat dry.

Coat the bottom of a large oven dish with olive oil. Overlap one layer of potato slices. Sprinkle with salt. Arrange the fish steaks over the top. Sprinkle with olive oil, salt and pepper.

Gloop together garlic, parsley, onions and herbs (use half as many herbs if you are using dried). Spread this mess over the fish. Then top with the halved tomatoes, cut side up. Sprinkle with lemon juice and olive oil and shove the dish into a 400° oven for 25 to 30 minutes.

THE CLAM CONNOISSEUR

CLAMS, OYSTERS, MUSSELS

IVAR THE CLAM CONNOISSEUR

Certainly I have nothing against the prevailing system of government in Seattle. However, I sometimes wondered if we wouldn't have benefited from an enlightened dictatorship with the late Ivar Haglund in the seat of command.

The first mention made of Ivar in the files of our morning newspaper establishes his credentials.

"Ivar Haglund to open cafe. Seeks parrot."

Naturally. Anybody intending to open a restaurant needs, in this order, (A) a stove, (B) a parrot, (C) some food and (D) some customers. I will admit I am a bit mystified by a second notation in the newspaper files.

"Ivar Haglund buys second octopus to replace one killed in bout with (one-time world heavyweight boxing challenger) Two-Ton Tony Galento." But it probably makes a lot of sense. Everything Haglund involved himself in usually did.

His civic campaigns urged a special issue postage stamp to immortalize the clam. He championed free cafeterias for seagulls. He exploded off thousands of dollars worth of fireworks for our enjoyment and his patriotic zeal. And he beautified our city by flying a glorious Japanese paper fish from the historic Smith Tower.

He wanted to put a clam in every Puget Sound pot and a smile on the kisser of every resident.

Know who first organized the International Pacific Amateur Free Style Clam Eating Contest Association in Seattle? Ivar Haglund, that's who. Richard Taylor of Bellevue won one of the most memorable contests, consuming 195 bivalves in eight minutes and between gulps, Ivar crowned the newly elected Miss Halibut Cheeks.

Shortly thereafter Ivar read an eastern Associated Press report acknowledging one Israel Weintraub of New Jersey as the world clam-eating champion.

``Imposter!" shouted Haglund. He demanded the presence of Israel Weintraub at the next IPAFSCECA eatoff in Seattle. Taylor retained his title by eating 337 clams in 10 minutes. ``World Champion" Israel Weintraub finished fifth. See, what Ivar Haglund represented was not only civic pride and betterment but moral indignation.

Ivar also sang his own commercials on television. He played a pretty bad guitar. He introduced tourists to alder smoked fish at his Salmon House on Lake Union. There are now a chain of seafood restaurants bearing his name. And his bronzed statue stands near the firehouse on the Seattle waterfront where one of his signs used to stand.

"It is OK to feed the seagulls. They have dainty appetites."

I don't know why the clam-eating tournament was discontinued, but a lot of us have been practicing diligently in case that competition is ever revived.

Personally, I prefer them steamed in a cup of dry vermouth, but these other dishes aren't half bad and are herewith dedicated to Ivar Haglund and Miss Halibut Cheeks, wherever she may be.

SEATTLE STEAMERS

clams (one pound per person)
1 cup water
1 cup dry white wine
1 onion, quartered
2 cloves garlic, sliced
1/2 cup chopped parsley
1 cube butter

Into your clam pot pour the water and wine. When hot add the clams, then toss in the onion, garlic, parsley and butter. Cover, steam and serve when all the clams have opened with mugs of the pot liquor on the side for drinking or dipping.

CLAMS BORDELAISE

4 tablespoons butter
2 mashed cloves garlic
2 cups chicken broth
1 cut dry white wine
3 dozen clams
4 tablespoons parsley
1 or 2 cups hot, steamed rice

Heat the butter in a large, heavy pan. Add parsley and garlic. Saute a minute or two. Pour in the chicken broth and wine and bring to a boil. Add the clams, cover and steam five to 10 minutes until they have opened.

Spoon rice into soup dishes, arrange clams in each bowl and pour broth over all.

DEBOB DEVILED CLAMS

1/2 cup chopped onion
1/2 cup chopped celery
1/2 cup chopped green pepper
4 tablespoons butter
2 tablespoons flour
1 tablespoon grated Parmesan cheese
1/4 teaspoon salt
pepper, Worcestershire sauce and hot pepper sauce (in bits and splats) to your taste
1/2 cup crushed Ritz crackers (12 crackers)
1 can (8 ounces) minced clams
another 1 tablespoon melted butter

In skillet cook the onion, celery and green pepper in four tablespoons butter until tender. Stir in flour, cheese and seasonings. Add 1/4 cup of the cracker crumbs and mix. Stir in the clams, undrained, and stir until mixture is thick and hot. Divide among two or three ovenproof bowls. Combine remaining crumbs and remaining butter, sprinkle over the top of each serving and bake in a 350° oven for 15 minutes.

HAPPY CLAMS

5 pounds clams
3 green onions, chopped
2 cloves garlic, minced
1 cup dry white wine
2 pinches thyme
2 tablespoons dry bread crumbs
1 dried red pepper

Coat the bottom of a large kettle with olive oil and saute the chopped onion and garlic, briefly. Dump in the washed clams, then the wine, thyme, bread crumbs and the chili pepper.

Cover and steam until clams open. Serve with the clam nectar and with melted butter on the side for dipping. Serves four.

RAINIER POOR BOY SANDWICH

1 pint oysters
3 tablespoons butter
1/2 cup chopped parsley
salt, pepper
4 ounces dry white wine
garlic bread, sliced

Drain the liquor from the oysters. Do not wash the little devils. Melt butter over low heat until bubbly. Add the parsley, salt and pepper to taste to the oysters and then pour the whole schmeer into the pan. Cook and stir frequently until oysters begin to firm. Add the wine and stir again. Cover and steam oysters just until edges curl. Serve over hot garlic bread or toast, to sop up the juices.

OH COME ALL YE OYSTERS STEW

1 large potato, peeled and sliced
1 large onion, chopped
3 stalks celery, sliced
1 frozen spinach souffle, thawed
2/3 stick butter
2 jars (10 ounces each) fresh oysters
1/2 pint heavy cream
salt, pepper
milk

Melt the butter in a pot and saute the potato, onion and celery until soft. Add the spinach, oysters and oyster liquor.

Simmer just until the edges of the oysters curl, then stir in whipping cream and enough milk to bring this stew to a desired consistency. Add salt and pepper to taste.

Heat but don't boil.

This will serve about four.

43

CLARICE'S OYSTERS

2 pints fresh oysters
1 large bunch fresh spinach
1 bunch green onions
2 stalks celery
1 clove garlic
4 tablespoons butter
1 tablespoon flour
1/4 cup cream
3 blips of Tabasco
1/4 teaspoon ground anise
1/2 teaspoon salt
grated Parmesan cheese

Arrange the oysters in a lightly greased, 12-hole muffin tin. Double up the oysters if you have more than 12.

Rinse the spinach, plop in a saucepan, cover and cook until wilted. Drain spinach thoroughly and then chop. Also chop the green onions and celery. Peel and mince the garlic.

Heat two tablespoons of butter in a skillet and saute the onion and celery. Stir-fry one minute and add minced garlic. Stir-fry another minute and add the spinach, then stir to blend.

Heat remaining two tablespoons of butter in a saucepan and add the flour. Blend with a whisk or spatula and when smooth stir in the cream and strained liquor from the oyster jars to make a cream sauce. Season with salt, anise and Tabasco. Add the spinach mixture and blend.

Spoon the resultant gluck over the oysters, sprinkle with Parmesan cheese and bake in a 450° oven for 20 to 25 minutes but DON'T OVERCOOK. This should serve four.

BEACON HILL BLUEPLATES

1/2 stick butter
3 minced green onions
1 clove garlic, lightly crushed
1 pint oysters
2 tablespoons chopped parsley
1/2 pound linguine or spaghetti
salt and pepper
Parmesan cheese

Plunk the butter into a skillet and when melted toss in the garlic clove. Let it sputter just until it turns golden and then throw away the garlic. Add the oysters (cut in half if they are large) plus the oyster liquor, the green onions and Parmesan. Reduce heat and simmer just until the edges of the oysters curl.

Toss with the pasta, which has been cooked in boiling, salted water. Season with salt and freshly ground black pepper and serve with two toasted hunks of French bread. This will serve two.

BEGINNERS BIVALVES

3 pounds mussels
6 tablespoons butter
4 green onions
1 large clove garlic
1 1/2 teaspoon dried basil
1/4 cup dry white wine
2 tablespoons brandy
parsley

Wash the mussels, cut off the beard and soak in salted water 30 minutes.

Gloop two tablespoons of butter into a large skillet. When melted toss in the minced garlic and green onions, chopped, tops and all. After three minutes dump in the mussels, basil and wine.

Cook over medium-high heat until the mussels open. Remove to a warm bowl with a slotted spoon.

Add the brandy to the pan juices and bring to a boil. Add the remaining four tablespoons of butter, in three pieces. When the butter is melted and the nectar is slightly reduced, slop everything over the mussels, sprinkle with parsley and serve. This amount will be adequate for two or three as a main course or four to six as an appetizer.

FAT CITY OYSTERS

3/4 cup dry bread crumbs
1/3 cup grated Parmesan cheese
1 teaspoon dried basil
1 teaspoon chopped parsley
1/2 teaspoon salt
1/2 teaspoon oregano
1/4 teaspoon pepper
1/4 teaspoon garlic powder
12 medium oysters (to serve two)
1 tablespoon olive oil
1 tablespoon white wine
1 teaspoon lemon juice

Preheat the oven to 400°. Grease a baking dish large enough to hold the oysters in one layer. Combine the crumbs, Parmesan cheese and the spices.

OK, sprinkle one third of the crumb mixture into the dish, top with the oysters and then spread the rest of the crumbs over the top.

Combine the oil, wine and lemon juice and sprinkle over the top. Bake uncovered for 30 minutes.

THE WATERFRONT

ALL SORTS OF SEAFOOD

THE WATERFRONT

He seems to be wearing an athletic supporter and a bicycle helmet. Clearly, he has become the bronzed symbol of the Seattle waterfront.

Granted, it is supposed to be Christopher Columbus and the inscription underneath the statue in Waterfront Park reads, "In the spirit of all voyages on the unknown sea."

But I can recognize a fitness freak when I see one. In recent years they have been attempting to take over the waterfront.

For a long time the sidewalks were filled from May to September with overstuffed tourists from Red Willow, Gosper and Hay Spring who would stop to peer into the steamed-clam tubs with expressions of pure horror asking, "Ya actually eat tham things, guts and all?"

These days, however, the tourists are doing the Spotted Pony Sidestep along the Seattle waterfront to avoid being trampled by sprinters, joggers and sloggers. The recreational runners hiss their way down the promenade with martyred looks.

They come pouring out of the large downtown bank buildings at 11:45, complete the loop run down to the end of Myrtle Edwards Park and back, then disappear at 12:45, sweating profusely. You can now understand why the downtown banks close early.

You only have to take one look at the gaunt form of C. Columbus to recognize that he is one of "them."

The probable reason that the pace has generally quickened along the waterfront is the suspicion that anybody who slows down will soon weigh more than the tourist from Hay Spring. Your senses are assaulted with mists and flavors rising from the seafood and hot dog stands. There are oysters and crabs and clam chowder and nectar fit for gods.

The Intermediate Eater recommends the alder-smoked halibut; the kielbasa with onion, hot mustard and dill relish at The Frankfurter; or a raid on one of the chicken stands or the pizza window at the top of the Pike Place hillclimb. Orrr, you can run five miles and finish your lunch hour with a carton of kumquat yogurt.

The tourist strip actually starts at the ferry terminal and ends at the Happy Hooker bait shop at the Myrtle Edwards Park fishing pier.

In between there is a first-class aquarium, scheduled volcano eruptions on the Omnimax screen, import stores, a merry-go-round, tour-boat harbors and a fountain which can satisfactorily drench an entire kindergarten class in 14.3 seconds. You can buy a burl table or a ship's compass. You might glimpse a fireboat, a freighter headed for the grain terminals or possibly a three-master training ship from Russia.

Meanwhile jets drone and helicopters sputter overhead and along the waterfront the ferryboat and trolley whistles play a two-note concert.

And the runners slide past headed for nirvana, which I think is located near Pier 66.

As for C. Columbus, well, he is clearly too pooped to plod which is why he has been resting at Waterfront Park for the last several years, leaning heavily on his sword. Obviously he needs a decent meal, and if he can't find some fish along the waterfront then he isn't much of an explorer.

He might have to look twice to spot smelt in a Pike Place fish market bin, but when they're running and fresh from the Cowlitz or Kalaloch Beach, they constitute a super breakfast for all the other waterfront athletes.

FAST-START SMELT

16 smelt
1 teaspoon salt
1/2 teaspoon pepper
1/2 cup cornmeal
1/2 cup flour
1/2 cup butter
3 tablespoons cooking oil

Clean the fish, cut off the heads, grab the backbone at the top part of the fish and pull toward the tail. All the bones should come out together.

Wash and dry the smelt, season with salt and pepper and roll in a mixture of the cornmeal and flour. Heat the butter and oil in a skillet and fry the butterflied smelt until golden on both sides. This will serve two.

SMELT FOR SUPPER

2 pounds fresh smelt
1 can beer
oil for frying
1 cup flour
1 teaspoon salt
1/4 teaspoon pepper
lemon wedges

Perform the same preliminary ritual described above to prepare the smelt. Pour the beer over the fish in a large bowl, cover with plastic wrap and chill for at least an hour.

Melt enough shortening or cooking oil to create a depth of about 3/4 inch in a skillet. Combine flour, salt and pepper in a pie plate.

Remove smelt from beer, roll in seasoned flour, dip again in beer, then again in flour. Fry the smelt in the hot oil, turning once, until golden on both sides. Drain on paper towels and serve with lemon wedges.

FIRST SETTLERS' SUPPER

2 pounds true cod steaks
1/2 cup Italian salad dressing
2 tablespoons lemon juice
1/2 teaspoon salt
1 can french fried onions
1/4 cup grated Parmesan cheese

Plunk the fish in a flat baking dish. Combine dressing, lemon juice and salt and slop all over the cod. Let them wallow in this muck for an hour or two, doing the backstroke.

Pour off the sauce and return fish to the dish. Crush the onions and mix with the Parmesan cheese. Gloop this glunk over the top of each steak and shove the dish into a 350° oven for 25 minutes or so. It will serve four to six as will the following.

A PLATE OF PISCES

2 pounds true cod
1 stick butter
1/2 cup olive oil
3 tablespoon wine vinegar
1 teaspoon dry mustard
1 teaspoon salt
1 teaspoon lemon juice
1/2 teaspoon basil
1/4 teaspoon pepper
1 clove garlic, minced
a few splats of Tabasco

Mix together all the ingredients except the fish and let burble for a minute or two in a saucepan, over medium low heat.

Fold some aluminum foil into a tray large enough to contain the fish in one layer. Brush the foil lightly with some of the butter-spice mixture. Set the foil on top of a broiler pan or cookie sheet. Plunk the fish on the foil, pour the sauce over the top and broil in your oven at the closest setting for four to eight minutes, depending upon the thickness of the fish.

FISCALLY SOUND FISH

1 1/4 pounds snapper
4 tablespoons dry white wine
1 lemon
4 slices bacon
pinches of parsley, garlic, thyme, basil
4 teaspoons chopped green onion
4 tablespoons butter

Cut two slices from the lemon and squeeze the remainder for juice. Cut the fish (to serve two) into 2-inch slices and place in a bowl with the white wine, lemon slices and a good grinding of pepper. Marinate for an hour then remove the fish from the gloop.

Rub oil on two pieces of aluminum foil. Put a slice of bacon on each hunk of foil, divide the fish between the two and then top with the other slices of bacon. Salt lightly. Then add the garlic and herbs.

Fold the foil to enclose the fish in a tightly sealed packet and bake in a 400° oven for about 15 minutes. While it is cooking add to the leftover marinade the green onion, butter, two teaspoons of lemon juice and boil down to reduce by half.

Serve the fish in foil packets and slop sauce over the top.

LING COD LOPEZ

2 bunches spinach
4 tablespoons butter
1/2 cup water
1/2 cup white wine
4 peppercorns
2 chopped green onions
4 cod fillets (about 1 pound total)
2 tablespoons flour
1/2 cup cream
dash of nutmeg
1/4 teaspoon lemon juice
salt, pepper
granted Parmesan cheese

Wash the spinach well, cook in some water and then dump it into a colander and press all the liquid out with the back of a spoon. Then chop coarsely and season the spinach with butter, salt and pepper. Create a spinach nest in four individual oven dishes and shove into a warm oven while you dirty some more pans.

Combine the water, wine, peppercorns, onions and more salt and pepper in a pan and let simmer for five minutes. Add the fish fillets and let simmer another five minutes, until poached. Remove the fish to a hot plate, bring the remaining liquid in the pan to a boil and after two minutes strain it and reserve.

In another saucepan melt two tablespoons butter and blend in the flour. Add the strained broth stirring, and keep stirring until this glunk thickens. Then add the cream, nutmeg and lemon juice.

Put a fish portion on each of the four spinach nests. Pour some wine sauce over each portion and sprinkle liberally with Parmesan cheese.

Then shove the four dishes into a 450° oven for five minutes, or until the cheese is lightly browned.

CHINA COD

2 pounds cod fillets
1/2 cup soy sauce
1/4 cup sugar
1/2 teaspoon Accent
2 tablespoons cooking oil
1 teaspoon granted ginger root
1 clove garlic, minced
1 tablespoon sesame seeds

In a bowl combine the soy, sugar, Accent, oil, ginger and garlic. Let fillets stand in this glunk for several hours.

Line a baking pan with foil. Lift fillets from soy mixture and place in a single layer in pan. Broil five to seven inches from heat for about four minutes, brushing once or twice with the marinade. Turn, brush again and sprinkle with sesame seed. Broil another three to five minutes until done. This should serve four.

RAINY DAY COD

2 pounds true cod fillets
2 teaspoons salt
1/2 teaspoon cayenne pepper
2 teaspoons minced ginger root
2 cloves garlic, minced
1/2 teaspoon turmeric
2 teaspoons ground coriander
1/2 teaspoon ground cumin
2 tablespoons lemon juice
4 tablespoons canola oil

Wash and dry the fish and cut the fillets into thirds. Mix together the salt, spices and lemon juice and pour over the fish. Let it marinate for 30 minutes.

Heat the oil in a large skillet. When it is hot lift the fish out of the marinade and pan cook on both sides just until done.

SEAHURST SNAPPER

1 pound snapper steaks
1 sliced onion
1/4 cup olive oil
1/2 teaspoon salt
1/4 teaspoon pepper
1/2 cup brown gravy
1/2 cup white wine
12 grated almonds
1 green pepper

Place the snapper on top of the sliced onion, which has been spread over the bottom of a casserole. Over the fish pour the mixture of oil, salt, pepper, gravy, wine and almonds. Top with the green pepper, seeded and sliced in rings. Bake in a 350° oven, covered, for 35 minutes. This will serve two to three.

WATERFRONT WHATEVER

3 pounds whatever (fish fillets of your choice)
2 cups fresh bread crumbs
1 cup sour cream
3/4 cup grated Parmesan cheese
1 1/4 teaspoon garlic salt

Moosh the bread crumbs, sour cream, Parmesan cheese and garlic salt briefly in the blender. Spread the mixture over the fish fillets which have been laid out like pixilated perch in a single layer in a large oven dish. Bake in a 450° oven for 15 to 20 minutes or until fish flakes when tested with that fork shaped like a mermaid which you bought on the Seattle waterfront. This should serve six or more.

THE KING OF CLAMS

CLAM CHOWDER & SEA STEWS

MONSTER OF THE DEEP

OK, so you've taken the vacationing relatives to the elephant house at the Zoo. They've seen the sea otters at the Aquarium. And they all said, "Here we gooooo!" on cue when the elevator started its climb up the Space Needle.

But they still haven't seen the single most spellbinding sight in Seattle, from the standpoint of the flatland visitor. It rests along about late springtime in an undistinguished bin at the Pike Place Market. And your cousin from Nebraska who has that little farm between Ong and Angus need take only one look and he'll holler at the top of his lungs:

"Gollleeee, Pauline. Come and look at this un!"

He has encountered the geoduck clam, an object of awe, ridicule and considerable controversy. You can't really describe the geoduck. You have to see it. All I can suggest is that if the geoduck were a movie, it would be off-limits to anyone under 18 who is not accompanied by a fish merchant.

Down through the years your fearless morning newspaper has on countless occasions served as an authoritative source on the geoduck. Clippings have been mailed to doubting friends and relatives at the other three corners of the country to prove the existence of a clam that will serve three or four at one meal.

Yet even when visitors to Seattle encounter it in the ... er, flesh ... they can hardly believe what they see. For that reason it remained on exhibit throughout the Century 21 Seattle World's Fair, and drew more whistles than the girlie show.

And in fact Northwest natives have also indulged in countless arguments and enormous tug-of-wars about and with this inscrutable bivalve. If you visit an ocean beach and are confronted by a resident's hind end you can surmise that he (or she) is locked in a death struggle with the giant clam. If you are a betting person, put $10 down on the clam.

Local historians tell us it was originally spelled Gweduc, then appeared as Goeduck and finally Geoduck in local logs and journals.

Legend had it that north coast Indians called it Geo Tuck, which meant, "of all clams king." But that was disputed by the Nisqually, who said the creature was called a Gwee Dukh and that the word meant "Deep Dig."

Actually, The Intermediate Eater has recently unearthed evidence that a Blackfoot Indian from Montana strayed into this territory, encountered the giant slug in a bin at the Pike Place Market and uttered the word, "Gggwwwuuuuuck!" And, of course, the meaning of that Blackfoot word is "double ugly," as in the tribal phrase, "I wouldn't touch that Gggwwwuuuuuck with a 12-foot cocktail fork!"

A have eaten Geoduck at a Pioneer Square bistro with Julia Child. The neck had been flattened, pounded, dipped in an egg wash then quickly fried in butter with a garnish of chopped nuts. It that form, it not only looks presentable, it tastes delicious.

Most first-time visitors to Seattle have only previously encountered the geoduck in cans ... chopped and indistinguishable. In that form, they probably don't care a fig about its historical background, as long as it can produce a chowder as good as this one.

GOE TUCK CHOWDER

4 strips bacon
2 onions, chopped
2 cups celery, chopped
3 medium potatoes, peeled and cubed
2 cups chicken broth
2 cans (7 oz. each) chopped clams
1 cup milk
3 tablespoons sherry
sour cream

Mince the bacon and cook in a frying pan. When the old grease begins to flow, toss in the onions and celery.

Meanwhile, plunk the potatoes into a saucepan containing the chicken broth and the liquid from the canned clams. Cook until the potatoes are soft, and smash 'em up with a North Coast Indian ritual war-club.

When the onions and celery are soft, glunk all the contents of the skillet into the saucepan with the potato puree. Add the cup of milk (more if you prefer).

Heat, add the clams and the sherry, heat again just below boiling point and ladle into soup bowls. Atop each one plop a big spoonful of sour cream.

This will serve four to six and will produce a wide grin on the faces of all but one of your guests. He's the guy with the farm between Ong and Angus, and he positively refuses to eat anything that didn't begin life with four feet.

A BOWL OF BOTTOMFISH

4 strips bacon, chopped
2 cups minced onion
4 cups fish stock or chicken broth
3 cups cubed potato
2 or 3 pounds cod or bass
4 cups half and half
thyme
salt and pepper

In your soup pot cook the bacon over medium heat. When it just begins to crisp, remove the bacon bits and to the fat remaining in the pot add the onion. When it has softened add the fish stock or bouillon, the potato, bacon and simmer over low heat for 20 minutes, or until the potato is soft. Add the fish, cut in hunks, and simmer five minutes.

Stir in the half and half, scalded, and add thyme, salt and pepper to taste. This will fill six large bowls and if you want you can add a hunk of butter and a scattering of parsley before serving. If you want to give this bowl of bottomfish an extra boost, stir in spoonfuls of spicy gloop to your taste.

SPICY GLOOP

2/3 cup of mayonnaise
2 minced cloves garlic
3/4 teaspoon cayenne
1 tablespoon white vinegar
1/4 teaspoon salt

FISH STEW SEATTLE

1 small onion, minced
1 can (No. 2 1/2) tomatoes
2 tablespoons chili sauce
1/2 teaspoon Italian herbs
1/2 teaspoon paprika
1 minced glove garlic
1/2 teaspoon salt
3 tablespoons olive oil
4 chopped stalks celery
1/4 teaspoon dry mustard
1 cup dry, white wine
2 carrots, chopped
1 tablespoons brown sugar
1/4 teaspoon celery salt
16 prawns
2 pounds clams in shells
1 pound red snapper
pint of clam nectar or chicken bouillon

Saute the onions and garlic in the hot oil in a large soup pot. When soft add all the other ingredients EXCEPT the fish, prawns and clams.

Let the stock simmer for at least an hour. Shell prawns and remove black vein from the back. Brush the clams under cold water to insure you don't have any booby traps (which act like clams, but actually consist of one tablespoon black sand).

When the hour is up, add the red snapper in chunks and toss in the prawns. Let the stew simmer another 15 minutes, then plunk in the clams. Cover pot, simmer another 10 to 15 minutes until all the clams have opened, then serve.

SHRIMP CHOWDER CARKEEK

1/4 cup butter
3 onions, chopped
3 stalks celery, chopped
1/2 green pepper, seeded and chopped
2 cloves garlic, minced
4 medium potatoes, peeled and chopped
4 small carrots, peeled and thinly sliced
1/2 teaspoon allspice
1/2 teaspoon basil
1/2 teaspoon turmeric
2 tablespoons Worcestershire sauce
2 tablespoons minced parsley
1/2 cup water
1 cup sweet vermouth
1 pound small, local shrimp
3/4 cup instant dry milk
4 cups whole milk
salt and pepper

Melt the butter in a heavy saucepan and saute the onion, green pepper, celery and garlic. Add the potatoes, carrots, herbs and spices, Worcestershire, parsley and water. Cover and simmer until potatoes begin to soften, at least enough to squash with a potato masher. Well, mash!

Add the vermouth, cover and continue to cook until carrots are tender. Add the shrimp and bring to a simmer.

Remove pot from the heat and stir in the dry milk and whole milk, a bit at a time.

Heat but don't boil. Taste, add salt and pepper as needed and this will serve about eight.

SHILSHOLE SALMON CHOWDER

1 quart water
1 teaspoon salt
2 cups diced celery and tops
1 large onion, diced
3 carrots, diced
2 large potatoes, diced
1/2 teaspoon basil
1 3/4 cups dry milk powder
1 can (1 pound) el cheapo brand salmon
1 tablespoon butter

All you do is to combine the water, salt, celery, onion, carrots, potatoes and basil in a large pot. Cook until vegetables are tender. Dissolve milk powder in a small amount of water and pour this sludge back into the pot. Dump in the salmon and break up with a wooden spoon. Simmer 10 minutes, taste to see if it needs more salt, plunk the butter on top and ladle into bowls.

CURRIED CLAM CHOWDER

2 cans clams
1 cup chicken broth
1/2 teaspoon thyme
1/2 teaspoon celery salt
1/2 teaspoon paprika
1/2 teaspoon pepper
2 large potatoes, diced
3 onions, peeled and chopped
5 strips bacon
1 tablespoon butter
1 teaspoon curry powder
1/2 cup dry white wine
3 cups milk
1/4 teaspoon cayenne

Heat the liquor from the two cans of clams in a saucepan with the chicken broth, thyme, celery salt, paprika and pepper. Add the diced potatoes.

Melt the butter in a skillet and add the bacon, chopped, and the onion. When the onions are soft stir in the curry powder and stir-cook two minutes. Pour this mess into the saucepan atop the other ingredients. Add the wine and simmer until the potatoes are tender. Toss in the clams, add the milk and cayenne or adjust to suit your personal thermometer. Add salt if needed. The chowder can be eaten at once but flavors improve overnight.

CORLISS COD CHOWDER

1 chopped onion
2 tablespoons olive oil
1 can (1 pound) tomatoes, chopped
2 cloves garlic, minced
1 strip orange peel, without the white pith
salt, pepper
pinch of turmeric
1/4 teaspoon fennel
1 pound cod
1/2 cup white wine

Heat the oil in your soup pot, toss in the onion and cook until it begins to smell like Walla Walla. Add the tomatoes, garlic, salt, pepper, turmeric, fennel and the orange peel. Simmer for an hour, covered.

Add a cup and a half of water and the half cup of wine. Remove peel, taste broth to see if it needs more seasoning or salt.

Adds the fish cut in chunks, cook another 15 minutes until the cod is just done, turn off the heat and let the pot sit, covered, for 10 minutes.

Rainier Avenue Cioppino

1/3 cup olive oil
1 large onion, peeled and thinly sliced
3 green onions, including green tops, chopped
1 green pepper, seeded and chopped
2 cloves garlic, minced
1/3 cup chopped parsley
1 can (1 pound) tomato puree
1 can (8 ounces) tomato sauce
1/2 cup dry, white wine
1/2 teaspoon oregano
3 teaspoons salt or to taste
1/4 teaspoon pepper
1/8 teaspoon rosemary
1/8 teaspoon thyme
2 Dungeness crabs
3 dozen clams in the shell
1 pound prawns, shelled and deveined

Heat the oil in a large pot and saute the onion, green onion, green pepper and garlic until the onion softens. Add the parsley, tomato puree, tomato sauce and wine. Refill the puree can with water and add this, too. Stir in all the seasonings.

Clean the crab and crack it too, removing enough hunks of shell so that the sauce can get to the crab meat.

Arrange crab pieces in your largest pot or roaster pan. Scatter the washed clams over the crab, scatter the prawns over the top and then pour the prepared tomato sauce over everything. Cover and simmer until the clams open, 20 to 30 minutes. Serves six second-generation Italians.

Scallop Bisque

4 medium tomatoes, quartered
1 onion, minced
1 stalk celery, sliced
2 carrots, sliced thinly
1/4 cup minced parsley
2 cloves garlic, minced
1 teaspoon basil
1 bay leaf
1 cup clam nectar or chicken broth
1/2 cup dry white wine
5 tablespoons butter
4 tablespoons flour
1 cup half and half
1 pound bay scallops
1/4 cup sherry
2 teaspoons fresh lemon juice
6 splats Tabasco
salt and pepper

Dump the tomatoes, onion, celery, carrots, parsley, garlic, basil and bay leaf into a saucepan. Cover with the white wine and the clam nectar or chicken stock. Simmer until the carrots and celery are as tender as sweetheart's caress. Remove the bay leaf, run this sludge through a blender, then force through a strainer.

In another saucepan, melt three tablespoons of butter, add the flour, and whisk in the half and half and the strained vegetable mixture. Cook, stirring, until it is smooth and has thickened.

Saute the scallops in two tablespoons butter just until they are no longer opaque. Dump them into the bisque mixture. Add the sherry, lemon juice, Tabasco and salt and pepper to taste.

This will make four to six servings, but if you want to extend it add more half and half and clam nectar, then adjust the seasonings.

Settler's Seafood Stew

1/2 cup olive oil
5 cloves minced garlic
1 1/2 pounds red snapper
flour
1 pound medium shrimp
1 dozen steamer clams
1 pound squid (calamari)
1 cup dry white wine
3 cups clam nectar
3 whole tomatoes, pureed
1/4 cup chopped parsley
salt, pepper
dash of cayenne pepper
3/4 teaspoon oregano

Cut the snapper in hunks. Clean the squid if you didn't buy it that way and cut into 1-inch squares. Shell the shrimp.

Heat the olive oil in a large pot and saute the garlic for a minute or two. Dip the snapper hunks in flour to coat, and brown in the pot. Then remove the fish chunks and set aside. Add to the pot the clams, wine, clam nectar, tomatoes and seasonings. Simmer about 10 minutes covered or until all the clams open. Return the snapper to the pot along with the shrimp and the squid. When the shrimp turn pink, dinner is ready. This will make about six bowls of seafood stew.

CHELAN CIOPPINO

1 cup chopped green pepper
1 1/2 cups chopped onion
1/3 cup olive oil
3 (14-ounce) cans Italian-style tomato chunks with juice
2 tablespoons tomato paste
1 1/2 teaspoons dried basil
1 1/2 teaspoons dried oregano
1 1/2 teaspoons dried thyme
2 teaspoons hot pepper flakes
1 1/2 cups chicken broth
2 cups red wine
1 1/2 pounds halibut
30 prawns
30 mussels

If you use clam nectar instead of chicken broth, this recipe instantly becomes Copalis (rather than Chelan) Cioppino. So watch yourself! You bear an enormous responsibility.

In a large pot heat the oil, then saute the pepper and onion. When soft add the tomatoes, paste, herbs, red pepper flakes, chicken broth and wine. Bring to a boil, lower heat and simmer 30 to 45 minutes. Shell the shrimp and toss into the pot along with the well-scrubbed mussels and the halibut, cut in chunks. Cover and simmer. The stew should be ready when the mussels open. Add salt if needed. If you prefer clams instead of mussels, add them to the pot first, then throw in the prawns and fish when the first clams start to open. This will serve six with lots of chewy Italian bread on the side for sopping up.

RENTON AVE. CIOPPINO

About 3 pounds canned, chopped tomatoes
1 can (1 pound, 14 ounces) tomato puree
1 package dry spaghetti mix
1 cup dry red wine
3 cups water
2 green peppers, seeded and cut in strips
2 large onions, chopped
8 cloves garlic, minced
1 bay leaf
1 tablespoon sugar
1 teaspoon oregano
dash of cayenne pepper
2 cans (13 ounces total) chopped clams with nectar
1 pound prawns, peeled
2 1/2 pounds fresh snapper, cod or other inexpensive fish

Dump into a large pot the tomatoes, puree, spaghetti mix, red wine, peppers, onions, garlic, bay leaf, sugar, oregano and two cups of water. Heat to a boil, reduce heat and simmer uncovered for two or three hours. Add all or part of the last cup of water as needed. Add cayenne in small pinches until the tomato stock is as peppery as you want it. Add salt if you want some.

Bring the stock to a slow boil again and add the clams and nectar. Then dump in the prawns and fish, cut in 1 1/2-inch hunks. When the fish is done (probably not more than five minutes) dish up into large bowls. This should be enough for six to eight helpings. Serve with a tossed salad and crusty Italian bread.

WILLAPA BAY CHOWDER

1 1/2 sticks of butter or margarine
2 onions, sliced
2 celery stalks
2 cups dry white wine
3 pounds mussels
4 medium potatoes
1 teaspoon dried basil
2 cups tomato sauce
2 cups cream
salt and pepper

Melt one stick of butter in a large pot. Add one-half onion sliced, one celery stalk sliced and the two cups of wine. Toss in the well-scrubbed mussels, bring to a boil and steam, covered, just until the mussels open.

Remove from the heat. Strain the liquid into a bowl. When the mussels are cool enough to handle, remove the meat from the shells and cut each mussel in half.

Melt the remaining four tablespoons of butter in a soup pot. Mince the remaining onions and the second stalk of celery and toss them into the pot. When the onions have softened, add the potatoes, peeled and cubed, plus the basil and simmer covered until the spuds are starting to soften.

Add strained liquid from mussel pot and the tomato sauce. Simmer until the potatoes are done. Add mussels and cream, plus salt and pepper to taste. When the chowder is hot (but not boiling) serve in six small bowls as a first course or in four big ones as the main dish.

THE WOODINVILLE WINERIES

PASTA

THE WOODINVILLE WINERIES

Every community should have such industrial blight. Granted the new manufacturing process brought Woodinville precious little poisonous ash, no oil slicks or odors of abattoir.

What it substituted instead were trout ponds, formal gardens, a carriage house and picnic area. And a virtually limitless fountain of the juice of the grape.

Granted the cows and pigs of the Snoqualmie Valley have not benefited from the Ste. Michelle winery, but that's their own fault. A by-product of the winery process, the dregs of the vast working vats is a potent mixture known as the lees. And in a lot of wine-making areas, the substance is fed to dairy herds or the residents of pig farms.

Wow, some cows were swearing off fodder. They'd belly up to the bar first thing in the morning and by noon were trying to ride bicycles, chasing cats back to the barn and picking fights with the electric milking machine.

At least that's what happened in California. Possibly because of the proximity of the Carnation Dairy complex, the Snoqualmie Valley cows wouldn't touch the stuff, and a lot of them have since given up chewing tobacco and cigars as well.

But if they are relatively unaffected by the wine industry, the rest of us have discovered a great way to spend an idle day.

Chateau Ste. Michelle, built on 87 acres once known as the Hollywood Farm estate, offers unguided strolls of the grounds, guided tours of the winery and a bit of the grape in the wine-tasting rooms.

There is also an outdoor concert area where symphonic musicians and bluegrass banjo plunkers have performed.

Just across from Ste. Michelle, in a picturesque Victorian house, is the showcase headquarters for Columbia Winery. It was founded in 1962 by a group of University of Washington professors who apparently decided to eliminate the middlemen for wine tastings in the Faculty Club.

The valley has been visited in recent years by the Spirit of Washington dinner train, which includes a stop at Ste. Michelle on the round trip from Renton to Woodinville. The chef turns out entrees like grilled salmon with cranberry chutney and Sichuan roast chicken breast. They even offer roast beef, if you dare to eat it in front of the Snoqualmie cows.

Guides at the winery will point out maps which show that the Yakima Valley, which produces their grapes, is located at almost the exact latitude as the Bordeaux and Burgundy regions of France. The guides will also point out to motor visitors or bicyclists from the Sammamish River trail where they can purchase a bottle or two of the best, plus some picnic cheese and sausages, if it's that time of the day.

It was that time of the day when we completed our tour. However, it was also raining generous buckets of wet outside so we grabbed a bottle of red and followed our noses to a simmering pot of spaghetti sauce at a nearby kitchen.

And the California cows think that THEY live in fat city!

Purple Palate Spaghetti Sauce

4 onions, chopped
1/4 cup butter
1/4 cup olive oil
4 cloves garlic, minced
1 1/2 cups chopped celery tops
1 green pepper, chopped
1/4 pound mushrooms, quartered
1 teaspoon basil
1 teaspoon rosemary
1/2 teaspoon pepper
2 teaspoons salt
2 pounds ground beef
1 can (1 pound, 4 oz.) tomatoes
1 can (6 oz.) tomato paste
1 cup dry red wine

Heat the oil and butter in a skillet and cook the onions until they start to relax. Dump in the garlic, stir-cook for a minute, then add the celery tops, green pepper, mushrooms and seasonings. Moosh everything around a few times while it cooks.

In your large spaghetti pot brown the hamburger, busting it up with a wooden spoon. When the last redness has disappeared from the meat, plunk all the sauteed vegetables into the pot. Give the tomatoes a couple of splurts in the blender and toss them into the pot, too, along with the tomato paste and wine.

Bring sauce to a boil, lower heat and simmer for at least two hours. Glooped over cooked spaghetti, this makes enough sauce to feed Woodinville.

Seattle Spaghetti

2 tablespoons olive oil
2 minced cloves garlic
1 teaspoon dry basil
1/2 teaspoon dry oregano
2 cups tomatoes, put through blender
1/2 cup chopped parsley
1 dried red pepper
12 pitted black olives
1 tablespoon drained capers
one-half of a 2-ounce can anchovies
clam juice or chicken broth
2 pound clams in shell
1/2 pound spaghetti
salt and pepper

Lightly saute the garlic in the hot oil. Dump in the herbs, tomatoes, parsley and the whole dried red pepper. Cook 30 minutes.

Add the olives, capers and the anchovies, chopped. Reheat and taste before adding salt and pepper. If this sauce is too thick for spaghetti, thin it with bottled clam juice or chicken broth.

Cook the half pound of spaghetti in boiling salted water. While that is burbling add the clams to the tomato sauce, cover and heat until the little buggers open their shells to take a look.

Ladle the spaghetti up into two large bowls. Top with sauce (discarding the dried pepper) and divide the opened clams among the two bowls.

This will serve Dorothy and Toto and any other two residents of Emerald City.

Seaside Spaghetti

3 tablespoons olive oil
1 onion, minced
1 clove garlic, minced
1/4 cup white wine
1 1/2 teaspoons dried basil
1 teaspoon dried marjoram
1 1/2 cups canned tomatoes, seeded and drained
1 fillet of sole
1/4 pound of small shrimp
salt, pepper
Parmesan cheese

Heat the oil in a saucepan over medium heat, add the onion and cook until soft. Add the garlic and cook another 30 seconds. Stir in the wine, basil, marjoram and cook a minute.

Now dump in the tomatoes and chop up with a wooden spoon. Increase the heat to boil the ingredients for five minutes.

Reduce the heat to medium, add the sole cut in half-inch hunks, plus the shrimp. Cover and cook two or three minutes until the sole is no longer translucent.

Serve over a half-pound of spaghetti, cooked in hard-boiling salted water for seven minutes or until tender to the tooth.

Sprinkle with salt and pepper to taste, a sprinkling of Parmesan and serve hot, on heated plates, to two panting gourmands.

FREMONT FETTUCCINE

1 small onion, chopped
1/4 cup olive oil
6 mushrooms, sliced
1/2 stick butter
2 ounces prosciutto ham, cut in thin strands
1/3 cup peeled, seeded and chopped tomato
1/2 of a chicken breast, skinned and cut in thin strips
1/3 cup cream
salt, pepper, nutmeg

Saute the onion in a skillet with the hot oil until it turns golden. Add the mushrooms and cook two minutes. Toss in the butter, the prosciutto, tomatoes, and cook six minutes. Stir in the chicken plus the cream. Bring to a simmer. When the chicken is done, taste and add salt, pepper and nutmeg to taste.

Serve over a quarter pound of green fettuccine (to serve two) which has been boiled in three quarts of salted water for about seven minutes. First drain and toss the fettuccine in a hot dish with two tablespoons of soft butter before topping with the sauce.

MADISON PARK MACARONI

3 tablespoons butter
1/4 cup minced onion
3 tablespoons flour
2 cups scalded milk
1/2 pound mozzarella cheese, grated
2 tablespoons minced pimento
3 Italian sausages
2 cups cooked elbow macaroni
salt, pepper
cayenne pepper to taste
1/4 cup grated Parmesan cheese
paprika

Melt the butter in a saucepan, saute the onion until soft, then stir in the flour and stir-cook for a couple of minutes.

Remove the pan from the heat and glunk in the scalded milk, whisking until it is smooth and thick. Return to heat and simmer the sauce 10 minutes.

Stir into the sauce the grated mozzarella, the pimento and the salt, pepper and cayenne to taste, and continue stirring until the cheese is melted.

into a buttered oven casserole plunk the cooked macaroni. Add the Italian sausages (I prefer the hot variety), which should have been simmered in water for 10 minutes, then sliced. Mix the macaroni and sausage with the cheese sauce, sprinkle the top with grated Parmesan and paprika and bake in a 350° oven for 45 minutes.

It will serve four.

SWEET SAUSAGE SAUCE

2 tablespoons olive oil
1 pound sweet Italian sausage
2 dried red peppers
1 can (28 oz.) plum tomatoes
1 cup minced parsley
2 cloves garlic, minced
1 green pepper
1/2 teaspoon oregano
salt, pepper
freshly grated Parmesan cheese

Heat the oil in a skillet, dump in the sausages, partially cover the pan and cook until browned on all sides, 15 to 20 minutes. Remove sausage to a warm dish and pour off all but two tablespoons of remaining fat in the skillet.

Toss the dried red peppers into the skillet over medium heat and when they turn black, throw them out the kitchen window.

Drain and chop the tomatoes and add to the skillet, along with the garlic and parsley and bring to a simmer. Reduce heat and add the green pepper (seeded and thinly sliced) oregano, salt and pepper. Cover and simmer over low heat 15 minutes, stirring occasionally.

Thinly slice the sausage and add to the pan.

Cook some pasta (about three-quarters of a pound for four servings) until just done, drain and toss it into the skillet. Add three tablespoons of Parmesan cheese, toss the pasta with the sauce and then serve, with more Parmesan in a side dish.

MOSS POINT MACARONI

1 cup uncooked macaroni
1 cup grated cheddar cheese
1 tablespoon Worcestershire sauce
2 tablespoons chili sauce
1/3 cup melted butter

Cook the macaroni, and while this is happening mix together the Worcestershire, chili sauce and butter.

Drain the macaroni and plunk on a hot platter. Sprinkle with grated cheese and sauce, toss until creamy and serve. It will feed two.

LAKE CITY LASAGNA

1 large onion, chopped
1 large carrot, chopped
1 stalk celery, chopped
1/4 cup minced parsley
3 minced cloves garlic
1/4 cup olive oil
1 1/4 pounds ground chicken or turkey
1/2 cup red wine
1 tablespoon tomato paste
2 cups hot chicken bouillon
1/3 pound thin sliced prosciutto
1/4 cup Parmesan cheese
salt, pepper, nutmeg
3/4 pound lasagna noodles

CHEESE FILLING

1/2 pound shredded mozzarella cheese mixed with
1 1/2 cups grated Parmesan cheese

CREAM SAUCE

1 cube butter
1/2 cup flour
3 cups milk
salt, nutmeg

Melt the butter in a pan, stir in the flour until smooth. Add milk slowly, stirring. Cook until smooth and thickened. Adjust the amount of milk to achieve a medium cream sauce. Add salt and nutmeg to taste.

OK, you're about ready to bust a gut on Lake City Lasagna. Saute the onion, carrot, celery, parsley and garlic in the olive oil until golden. Add the meat and saute 15 minutes, stirring to keep crumbly. Add the wine and cook another 15 minutes. Stir in the tomato paste, the chicken bouillon, prosciutto (or good grade of ham), salt, pepper and nutmeg to taste and cook another 15 minutes. Remove from the heat and stir in the quarter cup of Parmesan.

Meanwhile you should have been cooking the lasagna noodles according to package directions, dumping them into a tub of cold water when they are cooked.

Cover bottom of a 9-inch by 13-inch baking dish with some of the meat sauce. Top with some lasagna strips, top that with more meat sauce, then sprinkle on some cheese filling. Add another layer of pasta, slop in half the cream sauce, then the rest of the meat sauce and the rest of the noodles. Top with the last of the cheese filling and the last of the cream sauce.

Bake in a 375° oven until golden (about 25 minutes) let cook four minutes then cut into squares and serve.

The difference between very good and great Lake City Lasagna is to avoid using the already grated Parmesan available in the supermarket. Buy a block of good cheese and grate it yourself, just before you put the dish together.

CLAM ANCHOVY SPAGHETTI

1 or 2 cans clams, chopped
1/4 cup olive oil
3 minced cloves garlic
1/4 cup chopped parsley
1/2 cup white wine
8 anchovy fillets
3 tablespoons butter
2 chopped shallots
1/2 teaspoon rosemary
pepper
1 pound spaghetti to serve 4

Heat oil and butter in a skillet. Cook the garlic and shallots until golden. Add the anchovies and stir-cook until dissolved. Add the parsley, rosemary, clam juice from the cans and the wine. Bring to a boil and taste to see if it needs salt and pepper. Add the clams and cook five minutes. Serve over the cooked spaghetti.

BUTTE SPAGHETTI SAUCE

1/4 pound ground beef
butter
2 medium onions
5 stalks celery
1/2 bunch parsley
1 teaspoon pepper
1/2 teaspoon thyme
1/4 teaspoon cinnamon
1/4 teaspoon allspice
1/4 teaspoon cloves
1/8 teaspoon nutmeg
1 bay leaf
7 leaves rosemary
1/2 teaspoon basil
28-ounce cans tomato sauce
16-ounce can tomato paste
8-ounce can mushroom gravy
salt to taste

While singing a rousing Montana chorus of "On, Butte High School," brown the ground beef in butter.

Put the onions, celery and parsley through a grinder. I ran it through my food processor and got the same consistency.

Add remaining ingredients and simmer four hours, adding water as needed. When it's done, salt to taste and serve over Italian spaghetti marketed by a Tibetan company from grain grown six miles west of Great Falls.

PUTTANESCA SAUCE

3 tablespoons olive oil
4 cloves garlic, minced
1 onion, minced
2 28-ounce cans peeled Italian plum tomatoes, with juice
24 Calamata olives
2 tablespoons capers
3 1/2-ounce can anchovy fillets, chopped
1 teaspoon hot red pepper flakes
1 teaspoon dried oregano
2 tablespoons chopped parsley
salt to taste
freshly grated romano cheese

Buy the olives out of a bulk vat in an Italian deli. They cost too much by the jar. You want to cut each olive into four or five pieces, removing and discarding the pit in the process.

Heat the oil in a cooking pot. Cook the garlic and onion for about two minutes, until soft but not brown. Add the tomatoes and bust them up with a wooden spoon. Add the olive pieces, the capers, chopped anchovies, pepper flakes, oregano and one tablespoon chopped parsley. Simmer over low heat for about an hour, uncovered. Add salt to taste. You may not need any.

This is enough sauce for about eight portions of pasta, particularly bowtie or penne. Sprinkle on grated cheese and the rest of the parsley when you serve it up.

You might want to save some of the sauce and use it, at room temperature, as a topping for broiled fish or chicken breast. Or feed it to what's his name there in the highchair. The anchovies and red pepper flakes will give the kid a fast start on the culinary track.

GRACIOUS LIVING LASAGNA

8 ounces rippled-edge lasagna noodles
1 10-ounce package chopped frozen spinach
2 1/2 cups cooked turkey or chicken
2 cups medium cheddar cheese, shredded
1 can cream of mushroom soup
1 cup sour cream
1 can (4 ounces or more) sliced mushrooms, drained
1/3 cup minced green onions
1/2 teaspoon salt
1/4 teaspoon pepper
1/2 cup grated Parmesan cheese

In a large pot of boiling salted water, cook the lasagna until tender, about 10 minutes. Lay out the cooked pasta on pieces of waxed paper so it won't stick together and break up your marriage. Cook the spinach like it says on the box and drain well, squeezing out the excess moisture. Cube the turkey or chicken.

OK, got your mooshing apron on? In a large bowl, combine the turkey or chicken cubes with a cup and a half of the cheddar, the undiluted soup, sour cream, mushrooms, minced onion, salt and pepper. Well, don't just stand there. Moosh!

Butter the bottom and sides of an oven dish large enough to hold three strands of lasagna in one layer. After you have laid out the first layer, top with half the gloop in the bowl and sprinkle with 2 tablespoons of Parmesan. Top with three more pieces of lasagna, spread with the remaining turkey or chicken mixture and sprinkle with another two tablespoons of Parmesan. Top with the final layer of noodles, sprinkle with the remaining half-cup of cheddar cheese and the remaining quarter-cup of Parmesan.

Cover with aluminum foil and shove the dish into a 350° oven for 30 minutes. Remove foil and cook another 10 minutes or until golden brown and bubbly. Then remove from oven and let stand 15 minutes to firm up before you slice it. This should serve six normal eaters or four with hearty appetites. All you need to accompany the pasta is a heated loaf of sourdough bread, a tossed salad and a bottle of wine.

AUDUBON ITALIENNE

1 1/2 packed cups torn spinach leaves
1/2 cup chopped parsley
1/4 cup chicken broth
1 egg yolk
2 tablespoons Parmesan
1 teaspoon dried basil
3 cloves garlic
1/4 cup olive oil
3 half chicken breasts
3/4 pound pasta
2 fresh tomatoes

Skin and bone the chicken and cut into strips.

Dump the spinach, parsley, broth, egg, Parmesan, basil, garlic and olive oil in a blender and give it a blast until pureed.

The result should be a green gloop. If it is too thick, add more broth.

Cook the pasta and drain.

Heat some oil in a large skillet and saute the chicken about three minutes. Remove to a warm plate.

Dump the sauce into the same pan, cover and cook a minute or two. Add the tomatoes, cut into quarters and, when heated, toss the sauce with the pasta, serve up on four plates and scatter the chicken strips over the top.

This is also great if you use smoked chicken. I bought one at Larry's Market for about five bucks. It was already cooked, so all I had to do was cut the meat into strips and warm slightly in the microwave before adding to the pasta.

BALLARD

MEATBALLS & GROUND BEEF

BALLARD

See how educational this book has become? Up until now you probably never even suspected that the residents of Ballard ever drank any water.

Oh, they might be coaxed to inhale a little fruktvin or aquavit. But water?

Well, the fact of the matter is that the community of Ballard was swept into Seattle in 1907 on a tide of water, and I'm not talking about the opening of the Hiram Chittenden Locks.

Incorporated in 1890, Ballard was doing very nicely on its own after the turn of the century except for one minor inconvenience. The community relied upon well water, and when the fire laddies turned on their hoses there sometimes wasn't anything to drink for awhile. Except for fruktvin, aquavit and, oh, maybe a jigger of Bardahl.

Fortunately, a few years ago somebody learned how to brew a liquid known as Ballard Bitter. That ended the need for wells, a city water supply or rain, although they still get a goodly supply of the latter. A little precipitation never hurt anybody; and if it sometimes turns to sleet, well, that just reminds everybody of home.

Ballard, you see, became the state's Scandinavian center when fishermen and sawmill workers began to settle around what was originally known as Gilman Park. The lumber workers from the depleted forests of eastern America were attracted by the opportunities offered at almost 30 sawmills which once dotted the landscape. The fishermen, of course, were attracted by the herring and still put away a ton of it today, pickled, salted or sprinkled on their Fruit Loops for breakfast.

Did you know the rich used to ride to the hounds on the Harry Whitney Treat estate in north Ballard? Sure did. Today, for recreation, the residents of that area stand in smorgasbord lines, they engage in mating rituals along the beaches of Golden Gardens or they hike down to the Hiram Chittenden locks. There they can watch the new rich from Bellevue wrap ropes around their propeller shafts and swear at their wives, who are a step slow in splicing the yardarm to the mizzenmast when the water begins to run out of the lock.

An estimated two million visitors a year stand on the sides of the Ballard locks in the vain hope that a $200,000 yacht will someday disappear down the drain, cocktail flag fluttering from the stern.

There are two types of sweatshirt which sell particularly well in Ballard. One contains the message, "You can always tell a Norwegian, but you can't tell him much."

The other sweatshirts come in a set. One reads, "Quit shouting at me." The other reads, "I'm not shouting!!!" These sweatshirts were designed for the yachting couples.

The Chittenden locks, of course, connect Lake Union with the China Sea. Eventually.

Before attempting such a journey your average Ballard fisherman spends about two weeks in the smorgasbord lines trying to hook onto some meatballs like these.

MARKET STREET MEATBALLS

1 pound lean ground beef
1/2 teaspoon dried sage
4 tablespoons butter
1 tablespoon olive oil
1/4 cup grated Parmesan cheese
1 slice French bread
2 tablespoons milk
salt, flour
1/2 cup marsala wine

In a mixing bowl moosh around the meat, sage, a tablespoon of butter, salt and Parmesan. Cut the crust from the bread, soak it in the milk, squeeze and crumble it and hand-wrestle it into the other ingredients.

Roll the meat mixture into small meatballs and dust with flour.

Heat three tablespoons of butter and the tablespoon of oil in a skillet, brown the meatballs rapidly (don't overcook), slosh in the marsala and after a couple of minutes spoon the meatballs into a heated dish and pour the pan juices over all.

MORE BALLARD BALLS

1 3/4 pounds lean ground beef
1 teaspoon salt
1/4 teaspoon pepper
4 teaspoons steak sauce
1/3 cup dry bread crumbs
1 egg
2 tablespoons butter

With the exception of the butter, these are the ingredients you are supposed to moosh together to create about 18 meatballs. You'll also need:

2 more tablespoons butter
1/2 pound sliced mushrooms
2 tablespoons flour
1 teaspoon catsup
1 can beef bouillon, undiluted
1 package dry onion soup mix
1 cup sour cream

OK, after mixing and making the meatballs brown them in the melted butter in a large skillet. Reduce heat, cook another 10 minutes, then scoop the meatballs into a warm dish.

Add the other two tablespoons of butter to the skillet, dump in the mushrooms and stir-cook just until tender. Remove pan from heat.

Stir in the flour and catsup. Slowly add the bouillon, then dump in the onion soup mix, return to heat and bring to a boil, stirring as it thickens.

Return the meatballs to the pan, stir in the sour cream, moosh everything around over low heat and serve, over brown rice or noodles.

Obviously, Ballard residents do not survive on meatballs alone. Sometimes they invest their daily ration of ground beef in dishes like these:

GWEN'S GROUND BEEF 'N BEANS

2 pounds ground beef
2 onions
1/2 pound bacon, cut up
1 teaspoon salt
1 medium can Boston baked beans
1 medium can pork and beans
1 medium can kidney beans
1 medium can lima beans
1 cup catsup
3/4 cup brown sugar
2 tablespoons vinegar
1 teaspoon dry mustard

All you do is brown the hamburger in the same skillet with the chopped bacon and chopped onions. When browned, plunk into a casserole with the salt and all the other ingredients. Bake in a 325° oven for 45 minutes or until steaming hot.

CROWN HILL CASSEROLE

2 tablespoons canola oil
1 chopped onion
1 1/2 pounds ground beef
1 can mushroom soup
2 small cans tomato sauce
1 1/2 teaspoons salt
1/2 teaspoon garlic powder
1/2 teaspoon onion powder
1 teaspoon oregano
3/4 pound spaghetti, cooked and drained
1 pound sharp cheddar cheese, grated

Heat the cooking oil in a pot, stir-cook the onion until soft, glunk in the beef and cook until it no longer looks like home on the range.

Add the undiluted mushroom soup, the tomato sauce and the salt and spices and moosh everything round until hot.

Glunk half the noodles into a casserole, then top with half the sauce and half the cheese. Repeat layers of noodles, sauce and cheese.

Shove the casserole, uncovered, into a 325° oven for an hour or until the top is browned and crusty. This should serve about six.

LEARY AVENUE LOAF

1 1/2 pounds ground beef
1 1/2 pound ground veal
1/3 cup chopped green pepper
1/3 cup chopped onion
2 eggs
3 teaspoons salt
3 1/2 tablespoons bottled horseradish
3 tablespoons dry mustard
1/2 cup canned tomatoes, drained and chopped

LEARY AVENUE SAUCE

2 cans (8 ounces each) tomato sauce
1/2 cup water
3 tablespoons vinegar
3 tablespoons brown sugar
2 tablespoons prepared mustard
2 teaspoons Worcestershire sauce

Saute the onion and green pepper in a little butter just until soft and then moosh together with the meat (you can use all hamburger if you can't find ground veal,) the eggs, salt, horseradish, dry mustard and tomatoes.

Form into a loaf, plunk into a greased 9-by-5 loaf pan. Combine sauce ingredients and pour half of this over the top of the loaf.

Bake in a 350° oven for an hour and 15 minutes.

Heat the remaining sauce and pour into a gravy bowl so everybody can slop some over their slices of meat loaf.

SCANDINAVIAN STROGANOFF

1/2 cup minced onion
1 clove garlic, minced
2 tablespoons butter
1 pound lean ground beef
2 tablespoons flour
1 teaspoon salt
1/4 teaspoon pepper
1/4 teaspoon paprika
4 tablespoons dry red wine
1/2 pound fresh mushrooms
1 can cream of chicken soup
1 cup sour cream

Melt the butter in a skillet and briefly cook the onion and garlic. Toss in the beef and when browned add the flour, spices and the mushrooms, cleaned and sliced.

Cook five minutes then add the wine and soup. Simmer another 10 minutes, then stir in the sour cream. When hot serve over noodles, rice or mashed potatoes. This should be enough for four.

LOYAL HEIGHTS LOAF

1 stalk celery, chopped
1 onion, minced
1 carrot, minced
1 can (4 ounces) mushrooms, drained
1 green pepper, minced
1/2 teaspoon dry mustard
1/2 teaspoon salt
1/2 teaspoon sage
1/2 teaspoon garlic powder
1 tablespoon soy sauce
1 tablespoon Worcestershire sauce
1 cup milk
2 eggs
1 cup dry bread crumbs
1 1/2 pounds ground beef
1/2 pound pork sausage
tomato sauce

Combine all the ingredients except the meat, mix well and let stand 30 minutes. Add the meat, mix well again, and glunk everything into a greased bread pan.

Bake in a 350° oven for 75 minutes. Pour a small can of tomato sauce over the top for the final 15 minutes of cooking time.

MAMA'S MEATBALLS

1/4 pounds hamburger
3/4 pound ground lamb
1/4 cup minced parsley
1 large clove garlic, minced
1 teaspoon salt (or to taste)
1/4 teaspoon pepper
1/2 teaspoon dried oregano
3 green peppers
3 medium onions
olive oil
3 tomatoes, chopped
6 pitas
yogurt

Moosh together the beef, lamb, parsley, garlic, salt, pepper and oregano. Wet your hands with warm water and form the meat into 2-inch long "sausages."

Slice the peppers, discarding the seeds and white pith. Peel and slice the onions. Saute the onions and peppers in a skillet with hot olive oil until soft.

Broil, fry, or (best of all) barbecue the sausages over charcoal, in a hinged wire grill if you have one.

You can wrap sausages, peppers, onion, chopped tomatoes and yogurt into your warmed pita and eat as sandwiches. Or you can plunk the pita on a plate, top with the meat, vegetables and yogurt and eat with knife and fork.

PIONEER SQUARE

BEEF

PIONEER SQUARE

The idea was that Chief Sealth would sublet one of his pea patches adjoining Elliott Bay to the settlers from Alki Point. But the verbal contract made no allowances at all for Mexican Villages, comfort stations or clam nectar franchises.

Yet those have been principal items of contention influencing the history of that plot of ground now known as Pioneer Square, which houses some of Seattle's best shops, galleries and restaurants. Many of the world's greatest contemporary authors have read from their works at the Elliott Bay Book Company located in the center of the district. Some of them have written about the Native Americans who lived along this shore.

Chief Yellow Lark was a Delaware but claimed to be an expert on Siwash history and he insisted the land once constituted a sacred rest camp, offering an abundance of salmon berries and clams.

But settlers moved in, a sawmill was constructed, Yesler Way became known as Skid Road and there went the neighborhood.

By the turn of the century activity at Pioneer Place centered on the streetcar turnaround and some underground comfort stations, but they were all eventually closed. And 100 years after the Denny Party relocated in Seattle, Pioneer Square was the object of continuing controversy.

Restaurateur Ivar Haglund wanted to build a replica of the original Denny cabin as a clam nectar outlet. A Chamber of Commerce committee seriously considered transforming Pioneer Square instead into a Mexican village complete with adobe huts, strings of red peppers, burro carts and new restrooms marked Caballeros and Senoritas.

Maybe the existence of the totem pole discouraged that latter prospect. It is a replica of the original, which was either purchased or stolen by a group of Seattle businessmen during a visit to the Indians of southeast Alaska. For years it has been the social center for the street people of all races, who compare vintages while watching the procession along Skid Road.

To clarify, the term was originally applied to Yesler Way, because that was the route of the log skid from the sawmill to the bay. Eventually it was enlarged to describe First Avenue. These days it's a route taken by Seattle sports fans on the way to the Kingdome, which has housed more than one skidding franchise.

When the skidding gets tough the sports filberts congregate at watering holes like the Merchants Cafe, Sneakers, Duke's or F.X. McRory's, where the habitues drink out of glasses.

They also eat a lot of seafood, lamb chops and steak.

McRory's was opened in 1977 by Mick McHugh and his former partner, Tim Firnstahl. It was described then (and now) as "A great joint." The famed Whiskey Bar, reproduced in a Leroy Neiman painting which dominates the room, is noted for its selection of 152 different brands of bourbon.

Many locals were first introduced to McRory's as the terminus of the annual St. Patrick's Day Dash, a fun run which rewards a lot of entrants with celebratory Irish music and mugs of green beer.

When I'm on the financial skids and can't afford a hunk of beef at McRory's or the equally popular Metropolitan Grill, I find these to be perfectly acceptable substitutes for home consumption.

SKID-ROAD STEAK

a flank steak to serve four
2 cloves garlic
2 tablespoons soy sauce
1 tablespoon catsup
1 tablespoon cooking oil
1/2 teaspoon fresh ground black pepper
1/2 teaspoon oregano

Borrow a sharp knife from the guy who carved the totem pole and trim fat from the meat, then score the steak on both sides.

Mince the garlic and combine with the other ingredients. Rub this into both sides of the steak and let sit for 30 minutes. (If you have a very large flank you might want to increase the proportions of all ingredients.)

Broil the steak just until rare, then carve into thin slices on the diagonal and serve on hot plates.

BRANDY PEPPER STEAK

2 steaks, 1-inch thick
3 tablespoons peppercorns, crushed
5 tablespoons butter
1 tablespoon olive oil
1 ounce brandy
1/2 cup beef broth
1 teaspoon Dijon mustard
juice of a half lemon
3/4 cup sour cream

Crush the peppercorns and press into both sides of the steaks. Saute the meat in the oil and two tablespoons of butter for about two minutes on each side for rare. Remove meat from the skillet to a very hot plate. Add the brandy to the cooking juices and light. If you don't light it, it will taste like Hai Karate aftershave.

Now add the rest of the butter and the warmed beef stock and mustard. Add the lemon juice, stir, then boil to reduce the liquid by at least one third.

Then take the pan off the heat, stir in the sour cream, and when it begins to look like a sauce return the steak to the pan. Let it simmer one minute without boiling, and serve.

This will serve two, but you can obviously double the recipe. Matter of fact you might as well just leave the cork off that brandy bottle for a while.

If you want to barbecue or broil some flank or sirloin without marinating or if you just want to dish up some special ground beef patties these mushroom recipes produce excellent toppings.

MADRONA MUSHROOM SAUCE

1 pound fresh mushrooms
1 cup of onions, minced
1/4 cup butter
1 1/2 tablespoons Worcestershire sauce
1/2 tablespoon soy sauce
1/8 cup sherry

Thickly slice the mushrooms and saute with the onions in the butter for five minutes. Add the Worcestershire, soy sauce and wine and cook until the liquid evaporates enough for the sauce to thicken.

FOSTER ISLAND FUNGI

1/2 stick butter
1/2 cup onion, chopped
1 pound fresh mushrooms, sliced
1/3 cup dry vermouth
1 tablespoon Dijon mustard
salt, pepper

Melt the butter in a small skillet, cook the onions a couple of minutes and then toss in the mushrooms. When they lose their healthy look, glunk in the vermouth and cook, stirring, until most of the liquid has cooked off.

Remove the pan from the heat, stir in the mustard, add salt and pepper to taste and spoon over your steak or Fungiburgers.

REDMOND ROUND STEAK

2 pounds top round steak
3 tablespoons cooking oil
1 large onion, chopped
1 clove garlic, minced
2 tablespoons flour
1/2 cup chopped celery
1 can (8 ounces) tomato sauce
1 can (3 ounces) sliced mushrooms and broth
1 cup sour cream
1 teaspoon salt
1/4 teaspoon pepper
1 tablespoon Worcestershire sauce

Cut the steak into half-inch cubes and brown in the hot oil. Add the onion and garlic and cook until tender. Stir in the flour, then dump in all the remaining ingredients. Mix, gloop it all into a greased casserole and bake, uncovered, at 325° for 90 minutes. Serve over noodles.

FIREPIT FLANK STEAK

1 large flank steak
1 cup salad oil
4 tablespoons Worcestershire sauce
2 tablespoons dry mustard
2 teaspoons salt
2 teaspoons pepper
3/4 cup soy sauce
1/2 cup wine vinegar
2 minced cloves garlic
1/3 cup lemon juice

Plunk your steak in a flat Pyrex dish. Mix all the other ingredients and pour over the top. Let the steak marinate overnight or all day.

Cook the meat over a medium-hot barbecue fire (about five minutes on each side, but make a couple of test slices in the meat while it is cooking to be sure it won't be overdone).

While the meat is cooking let the marinade warm in a serving dish in a slow oven. Then when you slice the meat you can dump the thin cuts into the sauce. Otherwise they have a tendency to cool rapidly. You can let any leftovers sit in the sauce in the slow oven again, until everybody is ready for seconds.

PIKE PLACE STIR-FRY

1 pound round steak or flank
1/3 cup vegetable oil
1/3 cup soy sauce
1/3 cup vinegar
juice of one lime
1 package dry garlic salad dressing mix
1 large onion
1 large green pepper
2 stalks celery
additional vegetables
1 teaspoon honey

The additional veggies mentioned above should depend upon what looks good at the market today. You can add fresh spinach or zucchini, bean sprouts, bamboo shoots or water chestnuts. Whatever vegetables you use should be sliced thin.

Mix the vegetables, including the chopped onion and green pepper, with the soy sauce, vinegar, lime juice and the salad dressing mix. Slice the meat a quarter of an inch thick and toss into the marinade along with all the vegetables.

When you are ready to cook toss the meat slices (in three batches) into a hot, oiled skillet or wok and cook until browned, stirring. Remove to a warm plate.

With a slotted spoon scoop the vegetables, in one-cup batches, into the pan or wok and stir to one side when cooked. When you have cooked all the vegetables and just before serving, toss the meat

back into the wok and add all or part of the marinade and one teaspoon of honey.

Thicken with a tablespoon of cornstarch mixed with a quarter of a cup of water. Serve over Chinese noodles or cooked rice.

ALICE'S RESTAURANT SAUERBRATEN

4 pounds bottom round roast
1 sliced onions
4 cups red wine
1 cup water
3 tablespoons lemon juice
1/2 teaspoon basil
1/2 teaspoon thyme
3 whole cloves
4 peppercorns
1/4 teaspoon ground nutmeg

This is just for starters. Plunk the meat into a glass refrigerator bowl along with all the above ingredients, cover, and let it marinate the better part of a week, turning twice a day. (If you can't wait a week for dinner, open a can of ravioli but neither Alice nor I want to be implicated.)

When feast day arrives you will also need:

10 gingersnaps
1/2 cup butter
2 carrots, chopped
2 onions, chopped
2 ribs celery, chopped
some minced parsley
1 teaspoon salt
1/4 teaspoon pepper
1 tablespoon sugar

Melt the butter in a large oven pan, and after you have patted the roast dry with a paper towel brown it well on all sides, then remove.

Dump into the pan the carrots, onions, celery and parsley and stir-cook five minutes. Add the meat.

Strain that week-old marinade and slop it over the meat, too. Heat to a boil, cover and simmer until the roast is tender, about three or four hours, turning the meat a couple of times.

When the meat is done, remove to a warm platter. Pour the sauce and vegetables into a blender in batches along with the gingersnaps, salt, pepper and sugar. Whir until smooth and return to the pot. Stir-cook until thickened.

Slice the meat, pour the sauce over the top lavishly and serve to the board of directors of the Seattle German Club.

For the Daughters of Italy we'll need something different.

COW-PUNCHER'S PLATE

3 pounds thick cut round steak
3/4 cup sliced onion
1/3 cup red wine vinegar
1/4 cup cooking oil
1 garlic clove, minced
1 tablespoon Worcestershire sauce
1 teaspoon salt
1 teaspoon chili powder
1/2 teaspoon dry mustard
1/4 teaspoon pepper
1 tablespoon olive oil
1 can (8 ounces) tomato sauce
1/4 cup packed brown sugar
1/2 lemon, thinly sliced

This much steak should serve about eight. First you mix the onion, vinegar, oil, garlic, Worcestershire, salt, chili powder, mustard and pepper. Place steak in a flat dish, slosh the marinade over the top, cover with foil or plastic wrap and shove into the refrigerator overnight. If you are diligent you will set your alarm clock for 3 a.m. so that you can flip flop the meat in the sauce, because you want to perform this task three or four times.

When ready to cook, heat the shortening in a heavy frying pan. Remove the meat from the marinade and brown on both sides. Dump in the sliced onion from the marinade and about a third of a cup of the marinade. Cover the pan and simmer about two hours or until tender.

Remove beef to a warm dish. Skim off excess fat in the pan and add the remaining marinade, then the tomato sauce, brown sugar and sliced lemon. Simmer about 10 minutes.

Slice the meat thin, slop the sauce over the top and serve.

RAINIER BEACH BEEF ROLLS

1 1/2 pounds top sirloin or round steak
4 pieces thin-sliced ham (about 3 oz. total)
3 tablespoons grated Parmesan cheese
1 clove garlic
1/4 teaspoon sage
2/3 cup cooked and drained spinach
spaghetti
tomato sauce (recipe follows)

First you cut the meat into four hunks and then flatten each by pounding between two sheets of waxed paper with a 15th-century wooden Italian wine bottle.

Squeeze the spinach dry and combine in a blender or processor with the ham, garlic, Parmesan and sage. Spread this muck over the four flattened hunks of meat. Roll the meat slices and secure with toothpicks. Brown the meat rolls in an oiled skillet and then pour in tomato sauce and simmer 20 minutes if you bought top sirloin, 45 minutes to an hour if you used round steak. Remove the toothpicks and serve with cooked spaghetti and the tomato sauce.

TOMATO SAUCE

1 clove garlic
2 tablespoons olive oil
1 large can tomatoes
1 teaspoon dry basil
1/2 teaspoon salt
generous grinding of pepper

Cook the garlic clove in the oil until golden, then remove. Glunk in the tomatoes (I usually remove most of the seeds first) then add the seasonings and simmer 20 minutes, chopping up the tomatoes with a wooden spoon at the end.

BOGUS BUCO

beef or veal shanks to serve four
2 tablespoons butter
2 tablespoons olive oil
1 grated carrot
1 minced onion
1/3 cup chopped celery
1 cup beef bouillon
1 cup dry, white wine
2 tablespoons catsup
2 cloves garlic
1/2 teaspoon rosemary
1/2 teaspoon oregano
grated rind of one lemon
2 tablespoons chopped parsley
salt, pepper to taste
1 tablespoon flour

Heat the butter and oil in a skillet, brown the meat on both sides, then dump in the carrot, onion and celery. Simmer for 10 minutes, mooshing it around with a wooden spoon a couple of times. Add the wine, bouillon, catsup, one crushed clove of garlic, the rosemary and oregano. Bring to a simmer, cover and cook for an hour if you are using veal or 15 minutes longer if you have beef shanks. Taste and add salt and pepper as needed. Mix the flour with a bit of water and stir this into the pan juices to thicken slightly.

Chop the remaining clove of garlic, mix with the lemon rind and parsley, sprinkle this mixture over the top and you are ready to eat.

Sirloin Roast Robinwood

1 boneless sirloin roast
1/2 cup coarse black pepper
1/2 teaspoon cardamom seed
1 teaspoon catsup
1/2 teaspoon garlic powder
1 teaspoon paprika
1 cup soy sauce
3/4 cup vinegar

Rub the pepper and cardamom into the roast and let it sit, thinking deep thoughts, for 30 minutes.

Mix together the catsup, garlic powder, paprika, soy sauce and vinegar. Plunk the roast into a baking dish, slop the sauce over the top and refrigerate the meat overnight, turning several times in the marinade. Remove meat, reserving marinade.

Next you wrap the roast in foil and shove into a 300° oven for two hours.

When the meat is done pour any juices remaining into a measuring cup and skim off the fat. Add an equal amount of water. Heat and then add a few slurps of the leftover marinade to suit your taste.

You can slop this over the meat as is or you can thicken it into gravy by adding some cornstarch dissolved in water to the simmering sauce until it thickens. The meat should be carved in thin slices.

A Terminal Rump

a 5-pound boneless rump roast
2 cloves garlic
salt, pepper
1/2 cup chopped green onion tops
1 teaspoon basil
3 tablespoons chopped parsley
one or two cups beef bouillon

Peel and thinly slice one of the garlic cloves. Stab the roast a few times and insert garlic slivers into the slots. Salt and pepper the roast, plunk in a roaster pan and pop into a 325° oven until the meat thermometer yells that it's done.

Pour off the meat juices and save. Let the meat cool and then refrigerate.

When your stomach begins to growl, remove the roast from the refrigerator and slice as thinly as possible. Plunk the slices into a saucepan along with the onion, basil, parsley and the reserved pan juices, enough bouillon to cover and the other garlic clove, peeled and minced.

Heat at a simmer for 30 minutes and serve, maybe with some new potatoes or buttered egg noodles.

This will serve 10 to 12. If you have leftover slices, heat them in some more bouillon tomorrow and serve in split French rolls as sandwiches.

Royal Court Rump Roast

chuck or rump roast, 4 to 5 pounds
salt, pepper
2 chopped onions
2 diced carrots
1 cup chopped celery
1 teaspoon rosemary
1 teaspoon basil
1 cup dry white wine
1/4 cup white wine vinegar
1/4 cup brandy
2 cloves garlic, chopped

Salt and pepper the roast and place in a foil-lined roasting pan. Dump in the onions, carrots, celery, herbs, wine, vinegar, brandy and garlic. Cover the pan tightly or seal the foil around the roast to create a baking package.

Bake at 350° for two hours. Remove the meat to a warm platter, and when you have made the sauce cut the beef into thin slices and slop lots of sauce over the top of each serving.

The Royal Sauce

2 tablespoons butter
1 cup minced onion
1/4 cup flour
1 tablespoon crushed black peppercorns
1 cup half and half
2 tablespoons Dijon mustard
salt, pepper

Pour the pan roast juices into a blender along with the vegetable residue from the roaster. Give everything a whir.

In a saucepan heat the butter and cook the onion over medium heat about seven minutes. Stir in the flour, then blend in the gloop from the blender, the pepper, half and half and mustard. Stir-cook until it thickens, taste for salt (it will probably need some) and then start slopping it over the beef.

DINING OUT IN SEATTLE

PORK & LAMB

DINING OUT IN SEATTLE

It might give you a headache, except for the fact that the nervous system can concentrate on only one extreme pain at a time and your stomach is as empty as a bagpipe's bowels, and creating many of the same harmonics.

But where are you going to eat? Check the latest telephone directory. There are about 30 pages devoted to the listings of Seattle restaurants. By the time you make a choice, the bagpipe will be playing taps.

It wasn't that way in Seattle 25 years ago. It you were rich, you ate at Canlis. If you "merely made a nice living" you took the wife or family to Rosellini's 610. If you were down on your luck you ordered a bowl of red at Bob's Chili Parlor.

Everybody else ate at Von's.

Originally named Rippe's it was an institution for more than 50 years in Seattle, a 24-hour restaurant with a menu longer than the Dead Sea Scrolls and a kitchen capable of fulfilling each printed promise, thanks to a corps of sprinting, perspiring waiters.

Von's most famous client, during its later years, was fight promoter Jack Hurley who had his own stool at the end of the counter next to the kitchen.

Hurley was afflicted with rheumatism, sinus trouble, cataracts, and an ulcer operation had removed a third of his stomach. He didn't sleep a lot in the hotel room he rented permanently in the Olympic Hotel. But he appeared on somebody's counter stool regularly at 8 a.m., noon, 2 p.m., 4 o'clock, midnight and at 4 in the morning. And his snacks were usually consumed at Von's because on a slow night the waiters and counterman served as an attentive audience for Hurley's fistic recollections.

On a lot of occasions, down-on-their-luck managers or ex-boxers would follow Hurley from the Olympic lobby to Von's in hopes of a free snack. If they listened to enough stories, Hurley picked up the tab.

Hurley wouldn't have survived long today, under the golden arch or at the Kentucky Fried Colonel's. Those children behind the counter are supposed to serve 32 customers in a minute and a half. They wouldn't have time to listen to Hurley's story about the fighter who balked at having his purses split down the middle with his manager.

"How much you making now?" Hurley asked him.

"Nothing," the pug admitted.

"OK, then all I'm asking is 50 percent of nothing."

They liked that story at Von's Cafe and a whole generation of Seattle diners liked their food. It was so much a historic part of the Seattle dining scene that when Tim Firnstahl decided in 1988 to open an eating establishment in the heart of downtown Seattle he named it Von's Grand City Cafe complete with an efficient wait staff, lots of brass, dark woods, an enormous dawn-to-dusk menu and serious Manhattans and martinis.

It reinforces the tradition. However, if any of the short-order recipes survived from the original Von's, they haven't fallen into my clutches.

But this is the kind of rib-sticker food they once served.

PERKIN'S LANE PORK

a boneless pork loin, weighing 1 to 2 pounds
1/4 cup soy sauce
1/4 cup bourbon
2 tablespoons brown sugar

Mix the soy sauce with the bourbon and brown sugar, pour over the pork loin and let it vegetate overnight or all day in the refrigerator. Then shove it into a 325° oven for one hour, basting with the marinade. Carve the meat in thin slices on the diagonal and serve with:

MUSTARD SAUCE

1/3 cup sour cream
1/3 cup mayonnaise
1 tablespoon dry mustard
1 tablespoon chopped green onion
1 1/2 teaspoon vinegar
salt to taste

A POT OF PORK

5-pound boneless pork shoulder or butt roast
1/2 teaspoon fennel seed
1/4 cup flour
2 teaspoons salt
1 teaspoon pepper
1/2 teaspoon marjoram
1/2 teaspoon thyme
1/4 teaspoon nutmeg
oil
1 cup dry white wine
1 cup chicken broth
3/4 cup apple cider
2 cloves garlic, minced
1 cup sour cream

Crush the fennel seeds with the flour, salt, pepper, marjoram, thyme and nutmeg. Rub that critter lying there on the counter with oil and then massage it thoroughly with the seasoned flour. A little higher ... ah, right there ... boy that feels good.

Heat oil in a heavy pot, brown the pork on all sides, then dump in the wine, chicken broth, cider and garlic. Cover tightly and simmer the meat about 2 1/2 hours or until tender.

Remove the roast from the pot, boil the gravy to reduce by one third, then stir in a cup of sour cream and reheat.

Cut away the strings, slice the roast and let everybody slop some of the sauce over their serving, which might be accompanied by mashed potatoes and buttered carrots.

VON'S PORK CHOPS

4 pork chops
1 tablespoon oil
1 tablespoon Dijon mustard
1/2 teaspoon chopped garlic
1 egg yolk
1/4 pound grated Swiss cheese
1 tablespoon cream
1 tablespoon green onion tops
2 tablespoons dry white wine

Sprinkle the chops with salt and pepper. Heat oil in a skillet and brown chops on one side, about 10 minutes depending upon thickness of the meat. Turn and cook on second side until browned. Meanwhile you should preheat the oven broiler.

Blend the cheese, mustard, cream, garlic, chopped onion tops and raw egg yolk. Smear one side of the chops with the above mixture and shove under the broiler just until the topping is glazed.

Add the wine to the skillet, stir up all the brown nummies, add two tablespoons of water, bring to a boil, stirring, and pour over the chops, which have been served up on two warm platters.

POTATO-PORK PLATTER

1 can cheddar cheese soup
1/2 cup sour cream
chopped parsley
4 cups thinly sliced potatoes
salt, pepper
2 medium onions, thinly sliced
1 green pepper, chopped
6 pork chops
flour
2 tablespoons oil

Mix the soup with a quarter cup of water and moosh together with the sour cream and parsley.

In a large, shallow oven dish alternate layers of potatoes, sprinkled with salt and pepper, with layers of onions, green pepper and the soup mixture. Bake uncovered in a 375° oven for 30 minutes, which is how long it took Jack Hurley to tell a story at Von's.

While the spuds are cooking, dust the pork chops lightly with seasoned flour and brown on both sides in oil.

Remove the potatoes from the oven and stir lightly. Plunk the pork chops on top of the spuds in a single layer, cover dish and return to oven for 75 minutes, or until the spuds are tender to the fork.

LAKEMONT LOIN

a boneless pork loin weighing 1 to 2 pounds
1/2 cup sifted flour
2 tablespoons butter
1/2 cup sherry
1/4 cup water
1/2 cup chopped onion
1 clove garlic, minced
1 teaspoon salt
1/4 teaspoon pepper
1/4 teaspoon thyme
1/2 teaspoon oregano
2 cups fresh mushrooms, sliced

Slice the boneless pork tenderloin about an inch thick and then press with the palm of your hand to flatten. Dredge the pork in flour and brown quickly on both sides in a hot skillet containing the butter and oil. Glunk in the sherry, water, onion, garlic, the seasonings and herbs.

Cover the skillet and let simmer over low heat for 30 minutes, adding a small amount of water if necessary. Add the mushrooms and cook, covered, another 15 minutes.

PUGET SOUND PIGOUT

4 pound pork tenderloin roast
3 tablespoons salt
1/4 teaspoon pepper
1/4 teaspoon sage
1/4 teaspoon basil
generous pinch of allspice
4 cloves garlic
2 onions
2 carrots
herb bouquet (or mixed thyme and basil)
1/2 cup dry, white wine

Dump the salt, pepper, allspice and the quarter teaspoons of sage and basil into a sturdy bowl with two of the peeled garlic cloves. Mash this mess together with the butt end of a Heinie Manush-model baseball bat. Rub it over all surfaces of the pork roast and then let it sit all day.

When ready to cook brush off the excess coating. Pour four tablespoons of oil in a large pot and brown the roast on all sides. While this is happening peel and slice the onion and carrots.

Remove meat from the pot, pour off all but two tablespoons of oil and slow-cook the onions, carrots and two peeled, whole cloves of garlic. Toss in the herb bouquet, too.

After five minutes, plunk the meat back in the pot with the vegetables, fat side up, and heat until it begins to sizzle. Then shove the pot, covered, into a 325° oven for two hours, basting twice. (If you have a thermometer, it should read between 180 and 185 and call for clearing conditions with only a slight chance of rain over the Cascades.)

Remove the pork to a warm platter, add the white wine to the pot and boil the liquids down for a couple of minutes. Mash the vegetables into the pan juices and pour everything, unstrained, into a gravy boat.

If I'm cooking a pork roast, I peel and halve some potatoes, rub them with olive oil, sprinkle with salt and then plunk them into a pan and let them cook as long as the roast does, about two hours, turning occasionally and brushing with more oil as needed.

PASQUALE'S PEPPERS

6 large green peppers
2 tablespoons cooking oil
1 pound Italian sausage
1 pound lean ground beef
1/2 teaspoon salt
dash of pepper
1/2 teaspoon garlic powder
3/4 teaspoon oregano
1 can (15 ounces) tomato sauce
1/2 sauce can of water
6 slices white bread
3/4 cup grated Parmesan cheese
1/2 cup grated mozzarella cheese
1 teaspoon paprika

Cut the peppers in half lengthwise and discard the seeds and white pith. Parboil the peppers in water for five minutes, then drain and plop them into a large oven baking dish.

Heat two tablespoons of cooking oil in a large skillet. Remove the casings from the sausage and brown the meat. Add the ground beef and continue cooking until it looks more brown than pink. Pour off the grease.

To the meat add the salt, pepper, garlic powder, oregano, tomato sauce and water. Moosh everything together, bring to a boil, then reduce heat and simmer covered for 30 minutes.

Break the bread into hunks and toss into a bowl with the cheese and paprika. (I use hot paprika.) Add the meat mixture to the bowl and gluck everything together until well-mixed. Fill pepper with the mixture, heaping high. Cover the dish with foil, puncture with a fork in a couple of places and bake in a 350° oven for 40 minutes. Let it sit 10 minutes before serving.

You'll have 12 helpings, and I'll eat two of them myself.

Shanks for the Memory

4 lamb shanks
3 tablespoons olive oil
2 cups mushrooms, quartered
1 cup sliced carrots
1 large onion, coarsely chopped
1/2 cup sliced celery
4 cups beef bouillon
2 tablespoons catsup
1 clove garlic, minced
1/4 teaspoon pepper
1/4 teaspoon crumbled rosemary
1/4 teaspoon thyme
1 bay leaf

Heat the oil in a large skillet and brown the shanks on all sides, sprinkling the meat with salt and pepper. When browned, toss the legs into an oven casserole. Reduce the heat to medium and dump the vegetables into the pan, adding more oil if needed to saute them until they are soft and just beginning to brown.

Spoon the vegetables into the casserole with the shanks. Pour off any fat remaining in the skillet and pour in the beef broth. Add the catsup, minced garlic, the pepper and herbs.

Slosh all the broth mixture into the casserole and shove it, covered, into a 350° oven for 90 minutes.

Serve each guest one lamb shank and a mountain of mashed potatoes or cooked noodles and slop the broth mixture over everything.

Lamb Shanks Parthenon

6 lamb shanks
1/2 cup flour
1 teaspoon dried oregano
Salt, pepper
olive oil
3 chopped onions
2 cloves garlic, minced
1 cup beef stock
2 cups dry red wine
6 carrots, peeled and sliced
3 turnips, peeled and diced

Mix the flour with the oregano, salt, and pepper. Dredge the lamb shanks in the mixture thoroughly and then brown them in hot olive oil in a large pot. Remove the shanks from the pot, reduce heat and saute the onions and garlic for a couple of minutes.

Stir in two tablespoons of the leftover seasoned flour and cook two minutes more, stirring once or twice. Dump the shanks back into the pot and add the beef stock and red wine. Cover the pot and shove it into a 325° oven for about two hours. Add the vegetables, moosh everything around, then cover and return to the oven for a final 30 minutes.

Pine Street Pork

6 to 8 pork chops
1/2 cup water
1/4 cup vinegar
2 tablespoons dry mustard
3 tablespoons brown sugar
4 tablespoons chili sauce

Moosh together the water, vinegar, mustard, sugar and chili sauce. Season the chops with salt and pepper, place in a glass baking dish and then slop the sauce over the top.

Cover the dish and shove the chops into a 400° oven for an hour. Remove the covering, let bake another 30 minutes and serve.

Lake City Lamb Stew

4 pounds lamb stew meat
4 large Walla Walla onions
4 cloves garlic, minced
1/2 teaspoon thyme
2 bay leaves
1 teaspoon salt
good grinding of pepper
chicken broth
4 large carrots, cut in big chunks
6 potatoes, peeled and quartered
1 cup frozen peas

Cut the lamb into hunks. Peel the onions and slice 1/4-inch thick. Plunk the meat, onion, garlic, thyme, bay leaves, salt and pepper into a stew pot. Add sufficient chicken broth to cover.

Cover the pot, bring ingredients to a boil then reduce heat and simmer for 45 minutes, twice uncovering to skim any scum with an authentic Irish scum skimmer.

Add the carrots and potatoes, recover pot and cook until the vegetables are done. Remove and discard the bay leaves. Steam the peas in a saucepan until barely cooked and still firm.

Serve the stew in eight big bowls, sprinkle the peas over the top and serve with lots of freshly baked bread for slopping.

EASTER EVER AFTER

1 meaty lamb bone
1 quartered onion
2 large carrots, quartered
1 lemon slice
1 teaspoon salt
2 whole allspice
1/4 cup uncooked barley
1/2 cup diced celery
1/2 cup diced carrots
1/2 cup diced turnip
1 cup chopped leftover lamb
beef bouillon powder

Simmer the bone, quartered onion, quartered carrots, lemon, salt and allspice in two quarts of water for two hours. (If you don't have whole allspice, use 1/4 teaspoon of the powdered variety.)

Discard the bone, remove the meat and strain the broth.

Add the barley to the broth and cook 30 minutes. Add the diced vegetables and the leftover lamb, the meat from the bone and leftover lamb drippings or gravy, if you have any. Simmer another 30 minutes. Add beef bouillon powder, salt and pepper as needed.

PACIFIC PORK LOIN

boneless pork tenderloin
1/2 cup flour
1/2 teaspoon salt
1/4 teaspoon pepper
4 tablespoons olive oil
1/2 cup dry white wine
1/4 cup fresh lemon juice
2 tablespoons chopped parsley
1 teaspoon dried basil
1 teaspoon dried thyme
1 teaspoon dried oregano

A tenderloin weighing about a pound and a half will serve four to six. Carve it in half-inch ovals and flatten each one by pounding between moistened sheets of waxed paper. (You can also use veal scallops or uncooked and thinly sliced turkey breast instead of pork.)

Mix the salt and pepper with the flour and dredge the flattened slices of meat. Saute in hot oil, turning once, for about four minutes total cooking time. You may have to cook it in two batches, so remove the meat to a warm platter when done.

After you've removed the meat add the wine to the pan and boil it down to reduce by half. Add everything else, crumbling the herbs into the pan. Stir with a wooden spoon, scraping the bottom of the pan once or twice while this heats. Then pour the sauce over the pork on a large platter.

MAPLE SYRUP CHOPS

6 pork chops
2 tablespoons oil
1 teaspoon salt
1/2 cup maple syrup
1/2 cup catsup
splat of liquid smoke
2 tablespoons lemon juice
2 teaspoons Worcestershire sauce
1 tablespoon cornstarch mixed with 1/3 cup water

Brown the chops in oil, pour off any remaining fat. Mix the salt with the syrup, catsup, lemon juice and Worcestershire. Pour this glunk over the chops and simmer covered 25 minutes. Remove to warm platter. Pour cornstarch mixture into pan and stir-cook until thick, then pour over the chops.

SIXTH STREET SUPPER

1 1/2 pounds lean pork
2 tablespoons oil
2 tablespoons butter
2 onions
2 stalks celery
2 carrots
1 clove garlic
1 tablespoon flour
3/4 cup beef stock
1 tablespoon tomato paste
1/2 teaspoon salt
pinch of oregano
pinch of basil
freshly ground pepper
1/2 cup dry vermouth

For this dish you can use either wild South Sea Island boar or something like boneless pork tenderloin, cut in inch-size cubes.

Finely chop the onions, celery and carrots.

OK, saute the pork in oil and butter until brown, then remove from pan and keep warm.

Dump the vegetables and minced garlic into the pan, sprinkle with the flour and cook about five minutes, stirring frequently.

Mix the beef stock with the tomato paste and add this mess, too, along with the salt, pepper and herbs.

Return the meat to the pan, turn the heat down and simmer for 45 minutes. Add the vermouth and simmer another 15 minutes.

This should serve four with noodles that have been cooked in salted water, drained and tossed with butter and grated Parmesan cheese.

Ye Olde Curiosity Shop

Chicken, Turkey & Duck

YE OLDE CURIOSITY SHOP

"Just Arrived!" the sign outside read. "Mexican Jumping Beans."

To tell you the truth, it takes a whole lot of them to make a meal, but Ye Olde Curiosity Shop on Seattle's waterfront really isn't a grocery store at all. You can tell that just by looking at some of the clientele.

Leaning against one wall, for example, is Sylvia. She is 5 feet tall, but only weighs about 20 pounds. Standing next to her most days is her close friend, Sylvester, who looks like he hasn't had a square meal since 1895, the year his remains were found in the Gila Bend Desert.

But Ye Olde Curiosity Shop isn't just a hangout for mummies.

They've got a 10-pound geoduck, a pig with eight legs and three mouths plus a nekked-lady carving which would look great on the prow of your yacht. They've got Foo the Sacred Oriental Dog of Intelligence and fleas wearing dresses and ``one of the finest collections of shrunken heads outside of Ecuador."

They've also got 22,298 different items for sale that you absolutely do not need. But you'll probably depart the premises with a scrimshaw ring, a glowing-skull mask and a "I Hate Seagulls" T-shirt which seems to have been autographed by Big Bird from an altitude of 132 feet.

Thirty years ago there wasn't much of interest on the Seattle waterfront except for Ivar's Acres of Clams and Ye Olde Curiosity Shop, and the latter establishment has been mentioned in National Geographic, Vogue magazine and countless other periodicals.

The initial collection was carted from Denver to Seattle's waterfront in 1899 by "Daddy" Joe Standley, who correctly guessed that the Alaska Gold Rush would prove a boon to Seattle's prospects. But according to family historians total sales the first three days totaled 25 cents. Fortunately, that was also the price of a large salmon in that era, so Dad Standley's wife and four kids survived the few lean days.

Since then salmon have become more expensive than shrunken heads and the Curiosity Shop has been visited by Robert Ripley, General Foch, Edsel Ford and 97 trillion tourists' kids whining that, puleeeze, if they can only have some Mexican jumping beans they'll promise to feed 'em every day.

The first Curiosity Shop was located on Front Street, near the old Rainier Grand Hotel. It was moved to the original Colman Dock before The Big Fire, shifted again in 1963 to Pier 51 and in 1988 to make way for the enlarged ferry dock, it was relocated to its present location on Pier 54.

Talking about curiosities, I've got a few I might consider selling to Dad Standley's descendants if they didn't taste so good.

Curious? I'll say.

You know chickens don't fly.

I know chickens don't fly.

Chickens know chickens can't fly.

Yet I have a rare collection of chicken wings. Look 'em over quick. They won't last long when cooked like this:

Ye Olde Wing-Dinger

2 pounds chicken wings
1/2 cup plain yogurt
3 tablespoons lemon juice
1 tablespoon Dijon mustard
3 cloves garlic, minced
1 teaspoon salt
1/2 teaspoon sage
1/2 teaspoon oregano
1/2 cup dry bread crumbs
1/2 cup grated Parmesan cheese
cayenne to taste
melted butter

Cut the chicken wings at the two joints. Sell the tips to Ye Olde Curiosity Shop if you can get a good price. The meat on the other two bones from each wing is for eating!

Combine the yogurt, lemon juice, mustard, minced garlic, salt, sage, oregano and cayenne to taste and stir everything together with the tusk from a miniature elephant. Toss the chicken wings into this glunk, moosh everything around and then let it marinate covered at room temperature for a couple of hours or in the refrigerator if you want them to sit all day or overnight.

In a sack combine the bread crumbs, Parmesan and cayenne. Drain each wing bone, shake in the sack a few at a time, then space them out in a large, flat, buttered oven dish and shove into the refrigerator for an hour.

Preheat the oven to 375°. Drizzle melted butter over the wings then shove the dish into the oven for 40 minutes, or until golden brown.

Wow, these are good, even if chickens don't have wings. This recipe is a bit simpler but is also a winner.

Caspian Chicken

1 split broiler to serve two
1 cup rose wine
1/2 cup olive oil
2 teaspoons lemon juice
1/4 teaspoon thyme
1/4 teaspoon basil
1/4 teaspoon oregano
1/2 teaspoon MSG
1/4 teaspoon paprika
1 smashed clove garlic

What you do is to marinate the chicken halves in the above gloop from two to four hours. Then bake in a 325° oven for 90 minutes. Remove, salt and serve.

Betsy's Chicken

1 fryer
2 tablespoons butter
1 large onion
paprika
2 tablespoons flour
1/2 cup white wine
3 tablespoons sour cream
1/4 cup evaporated milk
noodles

Cut the chicken into serving-sized pieces. Peel and chop the onion.

Melt the butter in a large skillet, and when it is sizzling toss in the onions. Cook just until the onions start to brown then top them with the chicken pieces. Sprinkle with LOTS of paprika, then scatter the flour over the top. Pour the wine into the pan.

Cover the skillet and let the chicken cook over low heat for 45 minutes. Remove pan from the heat, stir in the sour cream and evaporated milk, then add salt and pepper to taste.

Spread the noodles, which have been cooked just until tender in salted water, over a large, heated platter. Top with the chicken pieces then slop the sauce over all.

Rare Oriental Fryer Flappers

2 to 3 pounds chicken wings
1/3 cup soy sauce
3 tablespoons brown sugar
3 tablespoons white sugar
3 tablespoons vinegar
1 tablespoon ground ginger
2 minced cloves garlic
1/2 cup strong chicken broth
MSG
freshly ground pepper

If you've got less energy today than Sylvester the Mummy, you don't have to do anything to the wings except toss them into a tub with all the other ingredients and let sit for three hours.

Place the wings in an oven pan and shove into a 350° oven for one hour or until dark brown, basting occasionally with the reserved marinade.

One note of caution. Last time I visited Ye Olde Curiosity Shop they were ``temporarily'' out of authentic shrunken heads. But they had them on reorder.

TASTER'S CHOICE CHICKEN

1 large chicken
6-ounce can frozen orange juice
6-ounce can of water
3/4 cup brown sugar
1/2 cup sherry

Cut the chicken into serving pieces and plunk into a casserole that provides a snug fit.

Mix the juice, water, sugar and wine in a saucepan. Simmer five minutes and pour over the chicken. Then all you do is to shove the uncovered casserole into a 350° oven and cook for 2 1/2 hours, turning a few times so that all the chicken will have the opportunity to brown on top. Serve the chicken with brown rice topped with a few toasted almonds because you'll have lots of extra sauce.

A MEAL FROM THE HEART

1 package frozen artichoke hearts
1 fryer chicken
1 onion
2 celery tops
1 cup grated medium cheddar cheese
1/2 cup white wine
1 cup white sauce

Just cook the hearts according to package instructions until just tender (or you can use canned artichoke hearts).

What you do with the chicken is to toss it into a pot of water along with the peeled and quartered onion, the celery tops and one tablespoon of salt. Bring the water to a boil, simmer 15 minutes, then turn off the heat and let the fryer sit in this hot tub for another hour, covered. When cooled remove meat and discard the skin and bones.

Spread the chicken meat over the bottom of a casserole, top with the artichoke hearts and pour over all the glunk made by combining the white sauce with the wine and cheese. Toss into a 350° oven until the sauce is bubbling.

CLE ELUM CLUCKER

1 best-of-fryer
1 teaspoon salt
1 teaspoon curry powder
1/2 teaspoon dry mustard
1/2 teaspoon paprika
1 teaspoon oregano
2 chicken bouillon cubes
1/2 cup boiling water
Tabasco (4 to 6 splats)
1 clove garlic
2 teaspoon Worcestershire sauce

Cut the chicken into serving pieces. (A best-of-fryer selection includes everything but the backs and elbows. If you want to reduce fat, you can remove the skin from the breasts and thighs.)

Place the chicken in an oven dish, meaty side down.

In a bowl mix together the salt, curry, mustard, paprika and oregano. Pour in the hot water, the bouillon, pressed garlic, Tabasco and Worcestershire. Stir until the bouillon is dissolved.

Spoon this glunk over the chicken. Bake the bird 30 minutes in a 300° oven, basting once. Turn over, baste again, return to oven 20 minutes, baste, turn heat to 400° and bake final 10 minutes.

STINKING ROSE CHICKEN

4 slices bacon
one cut-up fryer
2 onions, chopped
5 cloves garlic, peeled and smashed
1 1/4 cups dry white wine
2 tablespoons dry basil
1 teaspoon poultry seasoning
salt, pepper
1 tablespoon cornstarch

Although the above advises you to peel and smash the cloves, all garlic lovers know this is accomplished in one move. You put the garlic cloves under the flat edge of a large knife or clever, whack with your fist, then pick out and discard the husk and proceed to chop the garlic.

OK, spread the bacon slices out in a large skillet, cook until crisp, then drain on a paper towel.

Sprinkle the chicken pieces lightly with salt and pepper and brown in the hot bacon grease. Remove the chicken to the warmed hubcap of a 1967 John Deere tractor.

Now dump the chopped onion into the skillet and cook until limp. Add the garlic and stir-cook a minute. Spoon off any excess bacon fat at this point. Return the chicken to the pan and moosh some of the onion and garlic over the top of each piece.

Mix the wine with the basil, poultry seasoning, a half teaspoon of salt (or to taste) and some pepper. Pour this sludge over the chicken, cover the skillet and simmer about 45 minutes.

Plunk the chicken pieces on a warmed serving platter. Mix the cornstarch with one tablespoon of water and stir into the onion-wine mixture still in the skillet. Stir-cook until it has thickened into gravy and serve in a separate bowl to spoon over the chicken and the mashed potatoes.

Sure you need mashed potatoes. With gravy that good you need a portion about the size of Mount Si.

CHILBERG CHICKEN LIVERS

1 pound chicken livers
1 cup milk
1 teaspoon salt
pepper
3/4 cup flour
2 tablespoons butter
4 tablespoons olive oil
2 tablespoons red wine vinegar
2 tablespoons port wine
2 tablespoons chopped walnuts
2 tablespoons chopped chives

Cut away and discard the membrane holding together the livers. Don't give me that funny look. We could be having hog stomach for dinner.

Soak the livers in milk for 30 minutes, drain, pat dry with paper towels and dip to cover in flour which contains the salt and a fresh grinding of pepper.

Heat two tablespoons of butter and two tablespoons oil in a skillet. Cook the livers until crusted on both sides. You should finish this task in not more than five minutes of total cooking time for each batch. Remove the livers to a warm dish in a slow oven.

In a saucepan combine the other two tablespoons of oil with the vinegar, port and chopped nuts. Bring to a boil, dump in the chives and spoon this sauce over the hot livers. This should serve four.

CHICKEN A LA ALICE

2 chicken breasts
4 artichoke hearts
1/2 sweet red pepper
1/2 cup flour
1 teaspoon salt
1 1/2 teaspoons pepper
cooking oil
1 tablespoon butter
1 cup chicken broth
juice of one lemon

Skin and bone the whole chicken breasts, which should give you four portions. Quarter the artichoke hearts (we used the canned variety) and cut the red pepper in strips.

Mix flour with the salt and pepper. Dredge the breasts, then saute them in oil until they are golden brown on both sides. Remove them to a warm oven. Pour the oil out of the pan, add the butter, and when it is melted stir in a tablespoon of the leftover flour. Cook a minute, add the broth and stir-cook until the sauce is smooth and thickened. Add the lemon juice.

If you like a less tart sauce use the juice of only one-half the lemon. Add the artichoke hearts and red-pepper strips, cook another minute, then dish over the breasts. This is supposed to serve four, but Alice and I finished it all up. I have a modest appetite. But Alice really likes artichoke hearts.

TOTEM LAKE TETRAZZINI

1 large chicken
1/4 pound butter
8 tablespoons flour
1 cup milk
3/4 pound Velveeta cheese, cut in hunks
1 can ripe pitted olives
1/4 pound fresh mushrooms
3 ounces slivered toasted almonds
3 tablespoons minced onion
3 tablespoons minced green pepper
3 tablespoons minced celery
salt, pepper
8 ounces thin noodles, cooked

OK, first stew the chicken until tender, discard the skin and bones and cut the meat into bite-sized pieces and reserve the stock.

Heat the butter in a large skillet and blend in the flour. Slowly add four cups of the chicken broth, then the milk. Stir over low heat until thickened. Add the Velveeta and stir until melted. Toss in the chicken meat, the olives halved, and all other ingredients except the noodles.

Drain the cooked noodles and stir them into the chicken mixture, too. Turn into a large casserole and refrigerate until read to bake. Then heat it at 350° in the oven until the top begins to bubble.

This will serve eight to 12 members of the National Closet Velveeta Freak Society.

COLONIAL CHICKEN STRIPS

2 whole chicken breasts
one lemon
salt, pepper
1/2 teaspoon rosemary
1 clove garlic
1/4 cup olive oil
flour
two beaten eggs
bread crumbs

Skin and bone the chicken breasts and cut the meat into strips. Marinate for one hour in the juice of one lemon mixed with olive oil, a teaspoon of salt, one-quarter teaspoon of pepper, the half teaspoon of rosemary and the garlic clove, minced.

When ready to cook dry the chicken on paper towels, dip in flour seasoned with salt and pepper, then in beaten eggs and finally in bread crumbs.

Saute in more olive oil heated in a skillet, until the chicken is golden brown.

CHICKEN PASTA FOR SIX

6 chicken breast halves
1 1/2 cups marsala wine
2 tablespoons olive oil
1/2 pound mushrooms, sliced
1/2 cup chopped green onions
2 cloves garlic, minced
3 cups chicken broth
1 tablespoon lemon juice
1/2 teaspoon dried oregano
1/2 teaspoon dried basil
1/2 teaspoon salt
1/2 teaspoon pepper
1 1/2 tablespoon cornstarch
1 cup peeled, roasted peppers
dried pasta for six

Bone and skin the chicken breasts if you didn't buy them that way. Cut the breasts into strips and saute in the pan with a bit of oil until golden brown on all sides. Remove strips to a bowl.

Add wine to the pan, bring to a boil, then pour over chicken. Add more olive oil to the pan and add the mushrooms, green onions and garlic. Saute a minute, add 2 3/4 cups of chicken broth, the lemon juice, oregano, basil, salt and pepper. Add the peeled, roasted peppers, which you can buy in jars at most markets. Bring to a boil, then add the reserved chicken and wine.

Combine the final cup of broth with the cornstarch. When smooth, pour this into the pan and stir until everything thickens.

Divide the chicken mixture over six portions of pasta, which has been cooked just until done.

BURIEN BIRD

1 fryer, cut up
flour, salt and pepper
4 tablespoons olive oil
1 onion, chopped
1/4 cup ham, chopped
2 cloves garlic, minced
1 teaspoon dried basil
1/2 cup dry, white wine
1/2 cup chicken stock
1/3 cup pine nuts

The pine nuts are optional. To finance a bale of them at Costco you might have to sell your pickup truck with the rifle in the window. You can substitute slivered almonds.

Sprinkle the chicken pieces with salt and pepper, dredge in flour and skillet-cook in the hot olive oil until the bird is brown on both sides. Remove pieces to a warm place and cook the onion until soft in the same pan.

Add the ham (prosciutto is best), garlic and nuts and cook two minutes. Return chicken to the pan, dump in the remaining ingredients and cook, covered, at a simmer 30 to 45 minutes, or until done.

Dish the chicken up on a platter, pour the pan sauces over the top and serve. If you have a whole lot of pan juices you might want to remove the ham and onion bits with a slotted spoon and spread them over the chicken while you reduce the sauce over high heat.

CRYING FOWL

1/3 cup flour
1 tablespoon chili powder
1 teaspoon salt
1/2 teaspoon pepper
cooking oil
1 fryer, cut up
1 cup chopped onion
3/4 cup chicken broth
1/4 cup sherry
1/2 cup chili sauce
1/4 teaspoon garlic powder
1 teaspoon corn syrup
1/4 teaspoon celery salt
3 cups dried noodles

Mix together the flour, chili powder, salt and pepper. Coat each piece of chicken, and brown in hot oil in a large skillet. Plunk the bird in an oven dish.

In the same skillet saute the onions two minutes. Add the broth, sherry, chili sauce, garlic powder, corn syrup and celery salt. Simmer three minutes. Glunk this sludge over the chicken and shove the dish into a 350° oven for 45 minutes.

Cook and drain the noodles. Remove the chicken pieces to a platter. Dump the noodles into the dish the bird cooked in. Moosh the remaining sauces around with the noodles and this should serve four.

BRONZED BIRDS

6 game hens
1 clove garlic
1 teaspoon salt
1/2 teaspoon pepper
1/4 cup honey
1/4 cup whiskey
1/2 cup butter or margarine

Crush the garlic with the salt and combine with the pepper, honey, melted butter and the booze. Plunk the birds (they should weigh about a pound apiece) in an oven pan and brush with the booze butter. Cook in a 350° oven for 35 or 40 minutes, until done, basting a couple more times.

Three-Tree Point Turkey Dinner

1 large turkey, with giblets
2 cups chopped onion
2 sticks butter
3 cups chopped celery
1 cup chopped parsley
1 pint oysters
8 cups crumbled bread
2 cups chopped walnuts
2 teaspoons sage
1 1/2 teaspoon thyme
salt, pepper
1 cup dry, white wine
2 cups white sauce

Dump the giblets into a pan with three cups of salted water and simmer until tender, then chop the giblets and reserve the liquid. While that's happening lightly toast the crumbled bread.

In a skillet melt the two sticks of butter and saute the chopped onion over medium heat until softer than Priscilla's heart. Add the chopped celery and parsley and cook another five minutes. Let this muck cool.

Drain the oysters and chop coarsely, reserving the oyster liquor. Dump them into a large bowl along with the onion mixture, the crumbled bread, chopped walnuts, sage, thyme and salt and pepper to suit. Moisten the dressing with the oyster liquor and if you need more liquid add a bit of chicken broth.

Salt the turkey inside and out, lightly stuff and truss the bird.

Spoon remaining dressing into a buttered baking dish.

Spread a coating of butter over the turkey after you have plopped it on a rack in an oven roaster. Shove a thermometer into the thickest part of the thigh. Cook the turkey in a 325° oven about 14 minutes a pound, or until the thermometer reads 185°, covering the top of the bird with foil if it gets too dark. During the last hour of roasting, shove the casserole of extra dressing into the oven and cook covered for 40 minutes and uncovered for 20 more.

Pour most of the fat from the pan drippings. Add the wine and bring everything to a boil until the liquid is reduced by half.

Stir in the white sauce, add the chopped giblets, add salt and pepper to taste and call everybody to the groaning board. (You construct the white sauce by melting two tablespoons of butter in a pot, stirring in two tablespoons of flour, adding two cups of the stock and, when everything has thickened, flicking in a pinch of nutmeg.)

All-American Legs

6 turkey legs
1 cup flour
1 teaspoon salt
1/4 teaspoon pepper
1/2 teaspoon chili powder
6 tablespoons olive oil

What you do first is rinse the turkey legs and pat dry. Then dredge in the flour mixed with the salt, pepper and chili powder. Brown in a skillet with the hot oil, then dump some barbecue sauce over the drumsticks and simmer, covered, for an hour or two, basting frequently until tender. Oh, yeah, the barbecue sauce is constructed from:

1/3 cup vinegar
2/3 cup water
1 1/2 tablespoons prepared mustard
1/3 cup brown sugar
1/4 teaspoon pepper
1 teaspoon salt
pinch of cayenne pepper
2 lemon slices
1 large onion, minced
1/2 cup butter
2/3 cup catsup
1 1/2 tablespoons Worcestershire sauce

You combine all these ingredients and simmer 20 minutes before glooping it over the legs. This makes a lot of sauce, but that's a bonus if you are serving this with rice, noodles or mashed potatoes.

Leftover Turkey Casserole

4 cups leftover turkey, diced
2 cups chopped celery
2 cups toasted bread crumbs
1 cup mayonnaise
1/2 cup milk
1/4 cup chopped onion
1 teaspoon salt
pepper to taste
8 ounces swiss cheese, in strips
1 cup slivered almonds

All you do is combine everything except the almonds, spoon into a greased casserole, sprinkle with the nuts and bake covered in a 325° oven 30 to 40 minutes.

SHARPS' TURKEY

1 fresh turkey breast (4 to 5 pounds)
1 lemon
1/4 cup olive oil
3 cloves garlic
2 teaspoons dried basil
2 teaspoons dried thyme
1 teaspoon salt
1 teaspoon brown sugar
1/8 teaspoon black pepper

This recipe originated with local restaurant mogul Tim Firnstahl. The National Turkey Federation gave its New Product Award to the bird he serves at Sharps Fresh Roasting near the airport.

Firnstahl uses a two-day marinating process. We learned unexpected guests were coming and only marinated it about eight hours. It was still terrific.

What you do is to combine the juice from the lemon (saving the rind) with the olive oil, mashed garlic, basil, thyme, salt, sugar and pepper in a blender and whir for 15 seconds or so.

Brush the turkey breast liberally with this muck and don't neglect the cavity. Then shove the reserved lemon rind in the cavity and pop the breast into a large plastic produce sack. Tie the end and refrigerate all day or up to 48 hours. Remove the turkey from the bag. Brush the excess marinade from the sack over the breast again. Then you can roast the turkey in a 200° oven for three to five hours or until a thermometer stuck into the thick part of the breast reads 165°. Pour the defatted pan drippings over the slices of turkey when you serve it.

If you decide to barbecue the turkey breast instead shove it into a covered Webber over a medium hot fire, adding some wood to the charcoal occasionally to achieve a nice smoky taste. It will be done in an hour and 45 minutes. But use a thermometer to be sure you don't overcook the bird.

BIG BIRD DIJONNAISE

4 slices raw turkey breast
cooking oil
1/2 pound fresh mushrooms, cleaned and sliced
2 teaspoons Dijon mustard
pinch garlic salt
pinch of black pepper
3 ounces half-and-half
1 teaspoon butter

Heat in skillet just enough oil to thinly cover the bottom. Lightly brown the turkey slices on each side then remove to a warm platter.

Add to the pan the sliced mushroom, toss a couple of times with a spatula, then add all the other ingredients and heat to boiling. Pour this muck over the turkey slices and serve with a couple of slices of tomato on the side.

DIOGENES THE DUCK

1 domestic duck
1 1/2 cups orange juice
1/2 cup chicken stock
1/2 orange
1/4 cup port wine
1/4 cup currant jelly
3 tablespoons lemon juice
1/4 teaspoon ground ginger
cayenne pepper, black pepper and salt to taste

Salt and pepper the duck inside and out, then prick the skin in several places with a fork.

Cook the duck at 325°, allowing 25 minutes per pound, basting frequently with half a cup of orange juice mixed with the chicken stock.

While this is happening use a vegetable peeler to skin the half orange. You don't want any white part of the skin so don't carve too deep. Cut the peelings into slivers and simmer for three minutes in a bit of water.

After removing the duck from the oven, skim and discard the fat and pour the remaining juices into a pan. Add slivers of orange peel, the remaining cup of orange juice, the wine, jelly, lemon juice and spices. Simmer, pour into a sauce boat and serve to slop over the duck, which will serve two to three.

TACOMA TURKEY STUFFING

3/4 cup chopped celery
1 cup fresh, sliced mushrooms
4 tablespoons butter
7 onion rolls
1/2 teaspoon sage
1/2 teaspoon Italian seasonings
1 can undiluted cream of chicken soup
1 can undiluted cream of mushroom soup

Melt the butter in a skillet and cook the celery and mushrooms for a couple of minutes. Tear the onion rolls (you can usually find some in your supermarket and always in a Jewish delicatessen or bakery) into small cubes and plunk into a mixing bowl. Add the seasonings.

Dump in the soup, then the celery and mushrooms and mix thoroughly. This should stuff a 15-pound turkey.

SEATTLE CENTER

RIBS

SEATTLE CENTER

It was the spring of 1962 and certain employees of the Post-Intelligencer could be seen concernedly pacing off the distance between the front door and a construction project a couple of blocks away.

Since the average newspaper reporter cannot accurately compute the belt size for his trousers, the mathematical evidence they assembled in '62 was decidedly suspect. However, one thing is certain. The Space Needle hasn't yet fallen on the old P-I building, or the new one either. In fact it may be good for another 30 years. But there was a lot of skepticism way back then about the entire World's Fair project, including speculation that the Space Needle would bend at its hinges during the first strong wind and knock the P-I globe into Elliott Bay on one hop.

The Needle, of course, is now the city's most recognizable landmark and legacy from the Century 21 Exposition.

The fair drew 50,000 on opening day and before the gates closed almost 10 million admissions had been banked. The exhibits featured modern dynamos from Russia and ancient pottery from Peru. There were almost-nekked ladies in Gracie Hansen's Paradise International and the Old Vic Players performed in the Playhouse. The guy who caught Roger Maris' record-breaking home run ball tried to snag a horsehide dropped from the Fun Forest ferris wheel and chickens tried to peck out corn-producing codes in the Science Pavilion.

There was a Bubbleator and a monorail and masterpiece paintings and penny-pitch concessions. But mainly there was FOOD.

There was a French restaurant, and I know it was authentic because the cooks continually swore at the waiters through the swinging door. There was a Spanish village with flamenco and paella and an endless Food Circus menu that began with Mongolian steak and finished with Belgian waffles.

Well, you can still munch a Mongolianburger and order a ground fog of whipped cream on your waffle because the Food Circus yet survives, along with the Science Center, Coliseum and the Fun Forest in the 74-acre park and entertainment complex now known as the Seattle Center.

On sunny days a million screaming kids try to outguess a jillion water nozzles in the International Fountain, daring it to squirt them in the eye. And on cold, drippy days senior citizens swing and sway to Mood Indigo on the Food Circus dance floor.

The Center is the site of one of the biggest and most successful Folklife Festivals in the world. There are plant festivals, medical conferences, SuperSonic basketball games, and there is Bumbershoot, where you can listen to poetic readings or a rock band guaranteed to render you deaf in 37.6 seconds. You can also belly up to one of the countless food stands offering everything from falafel to fagiloi to foochow oolong.

The Intermediate Eater once served as a judge, deciding which applicants would be allowed to serve their food at the Bumbershoot festival. Of course, that meant sampling a bit of every food prepared by a day-long procession of chefs. I very nearly overdosed on fried oriental noodles, but rallied gamely at the first whiff of barbecue.

Gnawing on a barbecued rib is just about my favorite pastime when I'm not checking the Space Needle for structural weakness.

SPACE NEEDLE SPARERIBS

3 pounds country-styled spareribs
3 medium onions, quartered
2 carrots, sliced
1/4 cup vinegar
3 cups chili sauce
1 clove garlic, minced
1/4 teaspoon dry mustard
1 tablespoon A1 sauce
1 tablespoon Worcestershire sauce
1/4 cup brown sugar
2 cups beef broth
1/2 teaspoon allspice
1 teaspoon thyme
3 cloves
1 bay leaf

Brown the spareribs, carrots and onions under the oven broiler, turning spareribs, about 10 minutes on each side. Salt and pepper to taste. (So you hate washing the broiler. Nobody said this was going to be easy, Gladys.) Plunk the ribs into a large, rectangular oven dish.

Combine the chili sauce, garlic, vinegar, mustard, A1 sauce, Worcestershire and brown sugar in saucepan and simmer 10 minutes. Pour over the ribs.

Combine in a hunk of cheesecloth the allspice, thyme, cloves and bay leaf. Tie into a ball with a string and plunk in the center of the dish. Pour the bouillon over the ribs and the sauce and bake for 90 minutes at 350°.

This is Ethel Larue's recipe, and she says it'll serve six to eight, but I always eat a pound of ribs by myself.

THREE-HOUR SHORT RIBS

4 pounds short ribs
3 tablespoons cooking oil
1 1/2 cups chopped onion
2 minced cloves garlic
1 1/2 cups tomato puree
1/3 cup lemon juice
3 tablespoons Worcestershire sauce
2 tablespoons Dijon mustard
2 tablespoons firmly packed brown sugar
2 tablespoons red wine vinegar
1 tablespoon ground cumin
1 teaspoon salt
3/4 teaspoon cayenne

Sauce the onion in the oil, add all the other ingredients and simmer for five minutes.

Pour the sauce over the ribs and bake, covered, in a 325° oven for three hours, turning every 30 minutes.

Skim off the fat, dish up the ribs and slop the sauce over the top.

COLISEUM SHORT RIBS, SPAGHETTI

1/3 cup soy sauce
2/3 cup water
3 cloves garlic, minced
1 teaspoon grated ginger root
1/4 cup rum
2 tablespoons sugar
4 pounds lean beef short ribs
1/2 cup butter
1/2 cup sliced mushrooms
1/4 cup dry sherry
12 ounces spaghetti
2 eggs
1/3 cup grated Parmesan cheese
4 teaspoons cornstarch
4 tablespoons cold water

Moosh together in a bowl the first six ingredients. Sure, if you don't have any fresh ginger root you can use the powdered variety, but it won't be quite the same, Lester.

OK, what you are supposed to do first is to remove the meat from the rib bones. Slice the meat into thin strands and plunk into a pot with the sauce for 45 minutes, simmering, until tender.

Meanwhile in a skillet melt the butter and stir-cook the mushrooms until they lose that raw-earth look. Add the sherry to the mushrooms, bring to a boil and remove from the heat.

Cook the spaghetti until just tender in boiling salted water containing a bit of oil. Beat the eggs and cheese together until frothy.

Drain the spaghetti and plunk into a large bowl. Toss with the egg-cheese gloop and keep warm.

Stir the cornstarch-water mixture into the meat and cook until the sauce is thick. Dump in the mushrooms.

Scatter the spaghetti over a large, warm serving dish and top with the meat, mushrooms and sauce. This will serve about four.

MARMALADE RIBS

5 pounds meaty spareribs
1 cup soy sauce
1 cup orange marmalade
3 cloves garlic, crushed
1 teaspoon powdered ginger

This many spareribs will serve six and what you do is to mix the sauce, marmalade, garlic and ginger, pour over the ribs and let sit in the refrigerator for at least a day. Two days are even better.

Barbecue over a medium fire, turning and basting frequently, about 90 minutes.

HONOLULU RIBS

4 pounds short ribs cut in 2-inch hunks
3 tablespoons sesame seeds
1 large onion, sliced
1/2 cup soy sauce
1/4 cup packed brown sugar
2 minced cloves garlic
1/4 teaspoon ginger
1/4 teaspoon black pepper
cayenne pepper to taste
1 1/2 cups water
1 teaspoon cornstarch

Pick out an oven dish or pan that will hold the ribs. But first scatter sesame seeds over the bottom and shove into a 400° oven, just until the seeds are golden. Remove pan and over the top of the seeds place the rib hunks, then the onion slices.

Moosh together with a Seattle Center souvenir back scratcher the soy, sugar, garlic, ginger, black pepper, cayenne and water. Slop this over the meat, cover the oven dish with a lid or aluminum foil and return to the 400° oven until tender, maybe 90 minutes or two hours, stirring twice during the cooking process.

Plunk the meat onto a warm platter. Skim the fat from the pan. Mix the cornstarch with a teaspoon of water and stir this into the remaining pan juices. Stir-cook until it has thickened and pour it into a gravy boat so that everybody can slop some over their ribs. This will serve four to six and can be served with noodles or rice, plus glasses of genuine water from the International Fountain.

RIB-STICKER RIBS

5 pounds short ribs
1/2 cup flour
2 teaspoons salt
1/4 teaspoon pepper
2 cups onion, chopped
3/4 cup ketchup
2 tablespoons vinegar
2 tablespoons Worcestershire sauce
4 tablespoons soy sauce
1/2 cup brown sugar
3/4 cup water

Roll the ribs in flour mixed with the salt and pepper until coated on all sides. Place in a casserole and cover with onions. Mix together all the other ingredients. Gloop this over the ribs and cook in a 300° oven for three hours.

That's all there is to it. The ribs are great and should serve six to eight. You can use the same formula with good success to cook a pot roast.

FLAG-PAVILION RIBS

3 pounds pork spareribs
1 can tomato paste
2 chopped cloves garlic
1 tablespoon sugar
juice of one lemon
1 teaspoon salt
1/8 teaspoon pepper
1 cup water
1 tablespoon Tabasco sauce
1 tablespoon Worcestershire sauce
1 1/2 tablespoons chili powder
1/4 teaspoon onion salt

Plunk the ribs into salted water containing two split cloves of garlic and let simmer for 45 minutes, then drain and let cool.

Mix the other ingredients in a saucepan and simmer for about 30 minutes.

Preheat oven to 375°. Place ribs in a large, flat oven dish and baste the bone side of the ribs liberally with the sauce. Shove into the oven for 20 minutes.

Turn the ribs meat-side up and return to the oven for another 30 to 40 minutes, basting twice. Just before serving, spread the leftover sauce over the ribs and shove briefly under the broiler.

MARINER RIBS

3 tablespoons cooking oil
3 pounds lean short ribs
1 clove garlic
1 chopped onion
3/4 cup water
1/2 cup chili sauce
2 tablespoons soy sauce
1 teaspoon pickling spices

Cut the ribs into 2- or 3-inch hunks. Tie the pickling spices in a bit of cheesecloth or put inside a tea ball.

OK, along about the second inning heat a heavy pot, add the oil and then brown the ribs a few at a time. When they're all browned, pour off the excess oil, return the meat to the pot, add all the other ingredients. Cover and simmer until the game is over, about two hours.

During the post-game show remove and discard the pickling spices, add salt and pepper to taste and serve up the ribs on a big platter which in this instance we should call "home plate."

ELLIOTT BAY

STEWS

ELLIOTT BAY

It has been frequently but incorrectly reported that Elliott Bay was discovered in the year 932 B.C. by a Japanese explorer who docked at Pier 90 and immediately unloaded 3,000 Toyotas.

Actually, the bay was noted by Capt. George Vancouver in 1792 and first surveyed by Midshipman Sam Elliott of the Wilkes Expedition in 1841. He was attracted by the smell of oysters and chips from Ivar's and ended up buying a rattan deck chair and a Spanish wine skin at Trident Imports.

Elliott pronounced it an excellent harbor for a couple of reasons. Although 100 fathoms deep, sailors were able to run shrieking ashore from their ships, their feet barely touching the wave tops, because of a constant water temperature of 45°.

The best way to survey Elliott Bay today is from the deck of an excursion boat like the Goodtime III, which operates out of Pier 56.

What can you see?

Well, you can see Denny Hill, which doesn't exist any more. You can see Magnolia Bluff, which bears no magnolias.

The tour also offers a glimpse of the world-famous West Seattle magnetic bridge which exerts a pull on ships from 15 miles away until they eventually slam into the side and close all the commuter traffic corridors for seven to 10 weeks. At least that was the case with the old bridge. The new one is much taller and provides convenient collisions for much taller ships.

The Goodtime III also cruises past the Lockheed and Todd shipyards where on one typical tour we saw destroyers, frigates and ice breakers, recently returned from waters as cold as Elliott Bay, which has not yet been discovered by penguins.

The shipyards and the container cranes, which can unload nine million rattan deck chairs and 11 billion Spanish wine skins an hour, are all located on Harbor Island. According to the narrator on the Goodtime III, the 500-acre industrial island was created out of tide flats. It was built in part, he insisted, from the rock ballast dumped by old sailing schooners. Personally, I heard rumors that's where they buried Denny Hill.

Local historical archives contain pictures of giant pressure hoses blasting away at the hill with spouts of water, creating a perfectly flat landing strip for Buicks, Fords and Hudsons, which once occupied the Denny Regrade in a series of used car lots. Today, the real estate once occupied by Denny Hill is absorbing Seattle's downtown office building and residential expansion.

You see, Seattle used to be known as the City of Seven Hills but that distinction had previously been claimed by the Rome Chamber of Commerce. I'm not going to charge that some angry Italians put out a contract. All I know is that when the residents of Seattle woke up one morning they discovered Denny Hill had been tossed into Elliott Bay, wearing a pair of concrete overshoes.

Of course, Italy also gave us a lot of hard-working people who settled Rainier Valley and brought with them lots of tomatoes, garlic and vino needed to produce a variety of Puget Sound stews.

No-Brown Sloth Stew

3 pounds stewing beef in hunks
3 large carrots, in hunks
2 large onions, peeled and chopped
1 pound can tomatoes, drained
1 cup frozen peas
1 green pepper, seeded and chopped
1 cup red wine
4 tablespoons minute tapioca
1 tablespoon brown sugar
1/2 cup bread crumbs
1 1/2 teaspoons salt
1 teaspoon sage
1 teaspoon allspice
1 teaspoon basil
1 teaspoon thyme

Fling everything into a large pot, cover it and shove into a 250° oven. Then take a boat ride on the Goodtime III. After the stew has been cooking five or six hours remove yourself from the boat, the pot from the oven and serve.

Beer-Dumpling Stew

2 pounds beef chunks
flour
cooking oil
4 onions, peeled and thinly sliced
3 cloves garlic, minced
1 can undiluted beef bouillon
4 carrots, peeled and cut in chunks
1/4 cup red wine vinegar
3 tablespoons brown sugar
1 bay leaf
1 teaspoon thyme leaves
1 teaspoon salt
pepper to taste
1 can beer
1 1/2 cups biscuit mix
1/2 cup milk

Heat the oil in a skillet. Dredge the beef cubes in flour and brown on all sides over medium-high heat. Remove meat with a slotted spoon to a dutch oven.

Dump the onions into the pan, reduce heat slightly and cook, turning to prevent burning, until they are lightly browned. During the last two minutes toss the garlic bits atop the onions and stir everything around once or twice. Remove onion and garlic to dutch oven, too.

Pour the bouillon into the skillet, bring to a boil, scraping up all the brown nummies, and then dump this sludge into the beef-onion pot along with the carrots, vinegar, sugar, bay leaf, thyme, salt, pepper and beer. Stir to blend.

Shove the pot into a 325° oven for 2 1/2 hours.

Add the milk to the biscuit mix and stir thoroughly to create a soft dough.

Remove stew from the oven and place over medium-low heat on the stove. Drop the dough into the pot by spoonfuls and then let the stew simmer uncovered for 10 minutes. Cover, let it burble another 10 minutes, and by that time the dumplings should be done and you're ready to eat. This will serve four.

Columbia Park Stew

4 pounds stew beef
2 cups dry red wine
2 Walla Walla onions, sliced
2 tablespoons red wine vinegar
8 whole peppercorns
3 cloves garlic, smashed
1 teaspoon coriander seed
1 teaspoon thyme
1 bay leaf
4 strips orange peel, without any white pith
1/2 pound bacon
3 cups canned tomatoes, drained and chopped
1 pound carrots, sliced
1 pound mushrooms, quartered
1 pound small boiling onions
2 cups beef stock
2 more cloves garlic, minced
salt, pepper

Trim fat from the meat and plunk into a large bowl along with the next nine ingredients. Cover and marinate in refrigerator for 24 hours. Drain through a strainer, pushing the vegetables with the back of a wooden spoon to get as much of the liquid as possible. Discard the rest of that glunk sitting there in the strainer looking dismal.

Cook the bacon until crisp. Toss the beef cubes and marinade into a big cooking pot, top with the bacon, then the tomatoes, carrots, mushrooms and the boiling onions in layers. Add the reserved cloves of garlic, cover and simmer on top of the stove or in a medium-slow oven for two hours. Uncover and cook another hour or until the liquid is reduced, thick, rich and, golly, I can't stand it. Add salt and pepper to taste.

This stew is even better if allowed to sit in the refrigerator overnight, and thus is obviously also improved as a leftover.

GARFIELD GOULASH

4 tablespoons canola or olive oil
2 1/2 pounds chuck or stew beef in 2-inch chunks
3 large onions, peeled and chopped
4 teaspoons paprika
1 large clove garlic, minced
1 large tomato, peeled, seeded and chopped
1/4 teaspoon caraway seeds
1/2 teaspoon crumbled marjoram
1/8 teaspoon black pepper
1 bay leaf
3/4 cup red wine
1/4 cup water
1/2 pound ham, cut into 1-inch cubes
2 medium potatoes, cubed
1 cup sour cream

Heat two tablespoons of oil in the stew pot. Add the beef cubes and brown on all sides. Remove from pot. Plop in another two tablespoons oil, dump in the onions and stir-cook until tender. Return the beef to the pot.

Add the paprika, garlic, tomato, caraway seeds, marjoram, pepper, bay leaf, 1/2 cup of the wine and 1/4 cup of water. Cover and simmer slowly for two hours, stirring occasionally. (If you learn how to stir the stew without removing the top, send me a post-card.)

Add the ham (and more wine if necessary) and simmer for another hour. Add the potatoes and cook another 30 minutes, or until they are fork tender.

Remove bay leaf and discard.

Gloop one-quarter cup of the sour cream into the stew, mix and serve, with another spoonful of sour cream atop each portion. This serves six.

ST. MARK'S STEW

1 1/2 pounds veal or calf stew meat
3 tablespoons flour
3 tablespoons cooking oil
1 large onion, chopped
1/2 pound fresh mushrooms, sliced
1 teaspoon salt
1 envelope spaghetti sauce mix
1 can tomato sauce
6 carrots in hunks
3 medium zucchini, sliced

Coat meat with flour and brown in hot oil in a Dutch oven. Remove meat when browned. Add the onion and mushrooms to the pan and stir-cook until the onion is golden. Dump the meat back into the pot, add the salt, spaghetti sauce mix, the tomato sauce and two cups of water.

Simmer stew covered for an hour. Add the carrots, cook another 30 minutes covered. Add zucchini and simmer a final 20 minutes.

VINE ST. VEAL STEW

4 pounds veal shoulder, cut in cubes
1/4 cup butter
1/4 cup olive oil
2 teaspoons salt
1 tablespoon sugar
4 teaspoons curry powder
1 1/4 teaspoon pepper
1/2 teaspoon paprika
1 can (10 ounces) condensed beef broth
2 1/2 cups sour cream
2/3 cup flour
2/3 cup cold water
1 cup minced parsley
8 ounces spinach noodles
1/4 cup toasted slivered almonds
1 1/2 teaspoons poppy seeds

Two hours before you have planned indigestion, brown the veal cubes in butter and oil in three batches. Dump into a pot and sprinkle with salt, sugar, curry, pepper and paprika.

Chug-a-lug the broth into the pot and add the sour cream. Mix the flour with the water and stir this into the pot. Dump in the parsley. Simmer covered for an hour, stirring occasionally, until veal is tender.

Cook and drain the noodles while you heat the oven to 350°.

Arrange the cooked noodles in a ring around the edge of a shallow baking dish. Spoon the veal mixture into the center. Top with almonds and poppy seeds. Cover with foil, bake for 15 minutes and serve.

CINCHO SUPPER

2 pounds stew beef
1 package dry onion-beef soup mix
1 can mushroom soup
1 can (4 ounces) mushrooms, drained
1 cup ginger ale

Toss everything into a pot, cover tightly and cook three hours in a 325° oven, without removing the lid.

INTERNATIONAL DISTRICT

CHINESE AND ETHNIC FOOD

INTERNATIONAL DISTRICT

Our Chinese leader on that guided tour through the International District paused, after stops at the Wing Luke Museum and at an herb doctor's office. He pointed to a building across the street and informed the group of eight caucasians, "And that's where they make the fortune cookies you guys eat."

His inference was undoubtedly an accurate one. There are too many other good things to eat in the International District. Why should the residents who know better munch on a cardboard-flavored cookie containing a printed warning that reads:

"Beware of volcanos named Helen."

They don't need that. After all, if you know your way around the International District you can eat your way through some barbecued duck at the Kau Kau, some dim sum at the South China, sushi at the Mikado, sukiyaki at Aya's and maybe wander over to Inay's Kitchen for some Philippine pansit.

You can buy a hen at the China Poultry, a Dungeness at Live Crab Company and the Higo Variety Store offers 17 varieties of rice cookers.

You can purchase a chopping knife that will last a lifetime at Tashiro's Tools between stops at the Hen Sen Herbs and Korea Ginseng Co., while noting that the Kokusai Theater is showing Waka Oyabun Kenka Shiyo ("Young boss existing in the gambling world.")

As a young reporter at the P-I, I used to meet the family each Christmas Night at the Hong Kong, since I usually drew the holiday shifts. Most of the other downtown restaurants were closed but Chinatown was cooking on Christmas night, and my kids grew up thinking that braised spareribs with black bean sauce and pork fried rice were supposed to precede plum pudding on the holiday menu.

These days I positively cannot walk through the International District without making a left turn into Uwajimaya's.

On one visit I counted 128 different brands of noodles, 75 different cans or bottles of soy sauce. You could buy dried lotus root, microscopic little creatures labeled as "fragrant fish fried with pichled soybean." You can purchase quail eggs, fresh abalone, octopus, broiled eel, a Yukatas Kimono, a Siamese cookbook, Portuguese sausage, a $200 Kokeshi doll, a souvenir key chain, a Makunouchi food box or a porcelain saucer just six inches in diameter priced at $810.

You'll need a can of that and a sack of this and a lot of those because we're going to cook up a storm of Chinese and other ethnic food starting right about now.

King Street Teriyaki

1 fryer chicken
1/2 cup soy sauce
1/2 cup white wine
1/4 cup grated apple
1/4 cup grated onion
4 teaspoons toasted sesame seeds
1 tablespoon grated ginger root
pinch of MSG
Chinese noodles

Toss the cut-up chicken in a large bowl or plastic sack with the other ingredients and let it sit in your refrigerator, in a reflective posture, from eight to 48 hours, depending upon how hungry you are.

Then cook the chicken in a flat, oven dish placed in a 375° oven for 75 minutes, basting frequently. Remove the chicken to a warm platter. Pour the pan juices plus the remaining marinade into a saucepan and boil down to reduce.

Cook up some noodles, mix them with the sauce, plunk the cooked chicken on top and serve.

Alice's Walnut Chicken

2 chicken breasts
1 teaspoon salt
1 egg white
1 tablespoon cornstarch
oil for deep frying
1 cup walnut halves
1 sweet red pepper
1 green pepper
2 tablespoons black bean sauce
2 tablespoons sugar
1/4 cup chicken stock
1 tablespoon sherry

Skin and bone the chicken and chop into half-inch cubes. Mix them in a bowl with the salt, egg white and cornstarch. Then deep fry the chicken hunks in hot oil for two minutes and drain on paper towels. Next deep fry the walnuts in a strainer until golden brown and also drain on the towels.

Glunk two tablespoons of oil in a skillet or wok. Stir-fry the green and red peppers, cut into half-inch squares, for one minute and remove. Plunk the bean sauce into the pan and let it simmer three minutes. Lower the heat, add the sugar and cook for 30 seconds. Add the chicken stock and sherry and cook until sauce is dark brown.

Turn up the heat under the pan, add the chicken and peppers and stir-fry three or four minutes. Remove to a hot serving platter, scatter fried walnuts over the top and serve.

Sweet and Sour Soup

1/4 cup pork or ham, finely sliced
1 teaspoon dry sherry
3 tablespoons cornstarch
3 1/2 cups chicken broth
1/2 teaspoon salt
1 tablespoon soy sauce
1/4 cup dried wood ears
1/4 cup sliced bamboo shoots
1/2 cup bean curd, shredded
1 beaten egg
2 tablespoons cider vinegar
1/4 teaspoon white pepper
green onions

Mix the pork with the sherry and one teaspoon of cornstarch.

Wood ears are dried fungus bits which you can buy in most International District grocery stores. Soak them in boiling water according to directions, cover and let soak for 15 minutes. Snap off any wooden pieces from the wood ears. Wash, drain and squeeze out all the moisture.

Mix the remaining cornstarch with a half cup of water.

Put the vinegar and white pepper in a serving bowl.

Pour the broth, salt and soy sauce into saucepan. Bring to a boil and toss in the pork. Let it cook for a minute, then add the wood ears and bamboo shoots. Boil another minute, and add the bean curd. Boil again and stir in the cornstarch. Mix in the beaten egg, remove from heat and pour into the bowl containing the vinegar and pepper. Top each serving with a tablespoon of minced green onion and, as an optional addition, a teaspoon of sesame oil.

Chinese Chicken Salad

4 cups cooked and cubed chicken
2 cups chopped celery
3 green onions, sliced
2 pieces candied ginger, minced
1 teaspoon salt
1 1/2 cups mayonnaise
1/4 teaspoon curry powder (more if desired)
toasted slivered almonds
shredded lettuce

What you do is to mix the first seven ingredients, and refrigerate for at least an hour. Serve atop individual nests of shredded lettuce and sprinkle with the toasted almonds. That'll serve four generously.

HING HAY PORK

3 pounds of pork tenderloin
1/2 cup honey
1/2 cup water
2/3 cup soy sauce
1 teaspoon paprika
1 teaspoon dry mustard
1/2 cup barbecue sauce
1 teaspoon ginger
2/3 cup catsup
2 teaspoons salt
1/2 cup white wine
1 clove garlic, minced
1 teaspoon Worcestershire sauce

What you do is to let these boneless, lean tenderloins wallow around overnight in the glunk which you construct out of all the other ingredients.

Then bake, in the sauce, for an hour in a 350° oven, turning once after 30 minutes. Let cool, slice, and I like it as a side dish to a large bowl of Chinese noodles, served with toasted sesame seeds and hot mustard for dunking.

You can make your own hot mustard. Just mix dry mustard with some white wine until you have the desired consistency and let sit 30 minutes before serving.

This pork is also excellent chopped up in the noodles, or as an ingredient in fried rice, but if you dare serve it with canned chow mein, may the great Cathay Chicken lay a cracked egg in your Foo Young.

INDIAN CURRY CASSEROLE

3 tablespoons cooking oil
1 onion, chopped
2 stalks celery, chopped
1 green pepper, chopped
2 cloves garlic, minced
1 pound hamburger
1 tablespoon butter
1 tablespoon flour
1 tablespoon curry powder
1/2 cup milk
1/2 cup beef bouillon
1 teaspoon salt
1 cup uncooked quick brown rice
8 ounces tomato sauce
1 can (4 ounces) chopped green chilies
1 cup grated cheddar cheese

Heat the oil in a large skillet and toss in the onion, celery, garlic and the green pepper. Cook, stirring with a souvenir ruler from a Calcutta bank, until soft and then remove. Glunk the hamburger into the pan and when it has browned, pour off the grease.

In a saucepan melt the tablespoon of butter, stir in the flour and curry powder, cooking for one minute. Then pour in the milk, bouillon and salt and stir-cook until it thickens slightly. Meanwhile, prepare the rice to instructions on the package following the minimum amount of cooking time.

In a casserole gloop together the vegetables, hamburger, the curry sauce, tomato sauce, chilies, rice and a half cup of cheese. Top with the remaining half cup cheese and shove into a 350° oven for 30 minutes. This will serve four to six.

TACOMA TACO SALAD

1 1/2 pound ground beef
1 1/2 cups chopped onion
1 cup chopped celery
1 cup chopped green pepper
3 cloves garlic, minced
1 teaspoon salt
1 teaspoon chili powder
1/2 teaspoon cumin
1 large head lettuce
2 fresh tomatoes
4 ounces Fritos
1 can (10 ounces) tomatoes with green chilies
1 pound Velveeta cheese

Brown the meat in a large skillet and remove with a slotted spoon to a bowl.

To the remaining pan juices add the onion, celery, green pepper and the garlic. Dump the meat back on top of the veggies and add the salt, chile powder and cumin. Simmer 20 minutes. Chop the lettuce coarsely, dice the fresh tomatoes and dump into a large salad bowl. Slightly crush the Fritos and toss them in, too.

Dump the canned tomatoes with chilies into the top of a double boiler. (If you can't find this particular style of tomatoes use the same amount of medium-hot red chile salsa.) Cut the cheese into hunks, drop them into the boiler top and stir-cook until the cheese is melted and the mixture is smooth.

Add the meat mixture to the lettuce and fresh tomatoes in a salad bowl and toss everything around with two authentic Mexican chopsticks purchased at the souvenir store on South Tacoma Way.

This should serve about eight. Let everybody help themselves to a plate of the salad and then pass the hot cheese sauce around to slop over the top.

That'll grow a fur coat on a Mexican hairless.

ENCHILADAS ECONOMICO

1/2 cup chopped onion
1 clove garlic
1/4 cup oil, divided
2 cups diced cooked chicken
1 can (seven ounces) green chile salsa
1/4 cup canned chopped green chilies
3 teaspoons flour
2 teaspoons chicken bouillon base
1/4 teaspoon paprika
1 1/2 cups milk
1 1/2 cups shredded jack cheese, divided
6 corn tortillas

Heat a tablespoon of oil and let the onion and garlic sputter in a soft Spanish dialect until soft but not browned. Combine this glunk with the chicken meat, salsa and chopped chilies.

In a saucepan combine the flour, bouillon and paprika. Stir-cook while adding the milk slowly and continue stirring until it thickens slightly. Dump in a half-cup of cheese.

Heat the remaining oil in a skillet, heat the tortillas one at a time just until soft. As you slide each tortilla out of the oil, dip it in the cheese sauce, then plunk 1/3 cup of the chicken mixture down the center, roll up and place seam side down in a slightly greased baking dish.

When all of the enchiladas have been molded, folded and plopped, pour the remaining cheese sauce over the top, sprinkle with the remaining cheese and cover with foil.

Bake in a 350° oven for 15 minutes. Uncover and cook another 15 minutes. Serve when thoroughly heated and, if you like, you can pass around a bowl of homemade or canned red chile salsa to spoon over each helping.

CHINESE CHOPS

6 thick pork chops
1/2 cup white vinegar
3/4 cup honey
1/4 cup soy sauce
1/2 teaspoon ground ginger
1 clove garlic, minced

Moosh the last five ingredients together, pour into a dish that will hold all the chops in one layer, then toss in the meat. Marinate, covered and refrigerated, all day or overnight, turning a couple of times.

Remove from refrigerator and let sit for 30 minutes. Then bake covered, in the sauce, for 50 to 60 minutes in a 325° oven. If your chops aren't that thick, cut down the cooking time accordingly. You can serve this with rice or noodles.

KOTLETKI

1 pound hamburger
1 onion
2 slices bread
1 egg
cracker crumbs
1 can Campbell's consomme
2 tablespoons butter
1/4 pound fresh mushrooms (or more)

Peel the onion whole and grate it to make pulp, or chop in a blender until the last lump disappears.

Cut the crust off the bread slices, moisten the bread under a water faucet and squeeze. Throw it into a mixing bowl with the hamburger, egg, onion pulp and salt and pepper to taste. Mix thoroughly by hand until completely homogenized.

Form into six egg-shaped balls. Roll in crumbs and brown in butter which has been melted in a skillet. When golden brown, remove cutlets to a heated bowl, discard the fat but save the brown nummies in the pan. Pour in a can of consomme. Add a can of water and the sliced fresh mushrooms.

Turn heat to high, boil down the liquid slightly, stirring occasionally with a wooden spoon, then pour this nectar over the meatballs. After they have been allowed to perform the backstroke briefly in the bouillon serve, hopefully with mashed potatoes.

MAIN STREET MEIN

1 tablespoon butter
1/2 cup chopped onion
1 cup diced celery
1 (10 1/2-ounce) can mushroom soup
1 cup chicken broth
1 tablespoon soy sauce
few drops Tabasco
ground pepper to taste
2 cups leftover turkey
1 cup crisp chow mein noodles
1/3 cup cashew nuts

Melt the butter in a skillet, fling in the onion and celery and when they soften add the soup, bouillon, soy, Tabasco and pepper.

Add the turkey, stir-cook a minute or two, then dump everything into a casserole. Scatter the dried noodles and nuts over the top and bake in a 300° oven for 30 minutes.

GARLIC-SOY SATAY

flank steak (1 1/2 to 2 pounds)
1 tablespoon curry powder
1 tablespoon sugar
1/4 cup cooking oil
1/4 cup soy sauce
2 cloves garlic, minced

Cut the steak in thin diagonal strips. Combine the other ingredients, moosh together with the meat in a plastic bag and let it vegetate in the refrigerator all day or overnight.

Thread on satay sticks (which have been soaked in water), grill on the barbecue or under a broiler, and serve with this dipping sauce:

SATAY SAUCE

1/2 cup salted peanuts
1 medium onion
1 clove garlic
3 small dried whole red chilies
3 tablespoons cooking oil
1 teaspoon coriander
1/2 teaspoon cumin
6 ounces canned coconut milk
1 1/2 tablespoons brown sugar
1 tablespoon lemon juice
1 tablespoon soy sauce

Dump the peanuts into a blender or food processor and hit the button a couple of times until the goobers are finely chopped. Remove to a saucer.

Now toss the onion, in chunks, into the processor along with the garlic and chilies. Blend until smooth.

Heat the oil in a skillet, add the onion mixture, coriander and cumin. Stir-cook five minutes. Reduce heat to low and add the peanuts. Gradually stir in coconut milk, sugar, lemon juice and soy. Cook just below a simmer for 15 minutes.

JACKSON STREET NOODLES

1 bunch (about a pound) fresh spinach or 1 10-ounce package frozen spinach
5 tablespoons peanut oil
1/2 teaspoon red pepper flakes
1/2 cup plus 2 tablespoons chunky peanut butter
4 tablespoons minced green onions
3 tablespoons soy sauce
2 tablespoons vinegar
1 clove garlic, mashed
1 teaspoon sugar
1 pound Chinese egg noodles

Parboil the fresh spinach and drain until it is bone dry, or cook frozen spinach according to package directions.

Heat the oil and pepper flakes. (Add more flakes if your thermostat will accommodate three-star Oriental food.) Remove from heat and combine the oil in a bowl with the peanut butter, onion, soy, vinegar, garlic and sugar. Add warm water if the sauce needs to be thinned a bit.

Cook the noodles until done, drain, toss in a pan with the sauce and spinach, and when everything is warm serve to four or more refugees from Aurora Avenue.

FOURTH STREET FAJITAS

1 cup orange juice
1/2 cup vegetable oil
1/4 cup red wine vinegar
1/4 cup fresh lime juice
1 garlic clove, minced
1/2 teaspoon salt
1/2 teaspoon chili powder
1/4 teaspoon black pepper
2 pounds flank steak

OK, moosh together the first eight ingredients, then pour over the meat (trimmed of excess fat) and let it marinate, covered, in the refrigerator overnight.

You can barbecue or broil the steak to medium rare, then cut it in thin slices against the grain and serve with warm flour tortillas, grilled onions, guacamole and your favorite bottled Mexican red salsa or the one below.

SALSA PICANTE

1 16-ounce can whole tomatoes
2 jalapeno peppers, chopped
2 cloves garlic, minced
1 small onion, minced
2 tablespoons tomato paste
dash of cumin
1 1/2 teaspoons vinegar
salt to taste

Pour off the liquid from the can of tomatoes but reserve it. Then bust everything up in a blender and pour into a bowl. Add liquid from the tomato can until you get the consistency you desire. The leftover salsa keeps well in the refrigerator.

THE FERRYBOATS

DESSERTS

THE FERRYBOATS

The reason a lot of people who work in Seattle prefer to live in bizarre locations like Burton, Rollingbay and Colby is that they want to be able to swear at the ferryboats like everybody else in the office or plant.

It's a regional pastime. Sooner or later every Seattle resident considers island living. And a lot of people finally decide to make the big commitment and to lead the relaxed, laid-back lifestyle of a ferry-boat commuter. Then they spend the next three years of their lives standing on the dock at Winslow, Kingston or Vashon stamping one foot and swearing at ferryboats.

According to the people who rely on this form of transportation, the ferryboats are too expensive, too slow and the last one left two minutes ago.

It has been this way in Seattle since the first ferry went into operation, traveling from the foot of Main Street across West Seattle. Capacity was six loaded wagons and the fare was 15 cents. The customers immediately claimed it was too danged expensive, and the toll was lowered to a nickel.

Today there are more than 20 ferryboats in or out of operation on the average day and the biggest, like the Spokane and Walla Walla, can carry 206 autos and 2,000 passengers at 18 knots, once the commuters quit stamping their feet and climb aboard.

The Colman Ferry has been the center of commuter traffic since 1882 and through the era of the Mosquito Fleet. The other boats depart from Lincoln Park in West Seattle or from the picturesque communities of Mukilteo and Edmonds, where the laid-back residents view the frantic ferry commuters like they might observe the migration of the four-eyed flying smelt.

During the early 1900s they advertised a rubberneck ferry tour of "50 miles for 50 cents" around Bainbridge Island on the Hyak. Tourists who arrived here for the AYP Exposition or to see Teddy Roosevelt's Great White Fleet could board the Chippewa and travel to Orcas for a clambake on the beach, or take a $2 excursion on the Irraquois to Cape Flattery.

For a nickel, you could ride to Luna Amusement Park in West Seattle to view such wonders as the world-famous high-diving monkey and Professor Sylvan's balloon ascensions. During World War II, Boeing workers used to dance to the music of Jim Bowen and the Flying Birds on the moonlight cruises from Colman Dock aboard the Kalakala, "world's first and only streamlined ferryboat."

The Colman Dock was destroyed on a couple of occasions by fire, but when rebuilt its clock tower served as one of the city's most identifiable landmarks. One ill-fated night, however, the ferry Alameda went "go" instead of "whoa" and when it backed out from the dock the Colman clock was resting on its deck.

These days there is no Colman clock and not many spectacular accidents within the ferry system. However, if the 18 million people who ride the boats each year ever decide to stamp their feet in unison, Vashon, Bainbridge and Whidbey islands are all going to sink permanently from view.

BURTON BLUEBERRY PIE

pastry for a two-crust pie
2/3 cup sugar
3 tablespoons flour
1/2 teaspoon grated lemon rind
2 teaspoons lemon juice
1/4 teaspoon nutmeg
1/2 teaspoon cinnamon
1/4 teaspoon salt
4 cups fresh or frozen blueberries (not in syrup)
1 tablespoon butter
light cream and sugar for glaze

Line pie plate with pastry. Mix sugar with flour, lemon rind and juice, spices and salt. Place half of the berries in pie plate and sprinkle with half the sugar mixture. Repeat, dot with butter.

Roll out the top crust and place over the pie. Cut four slits near the center. Glaze by brushing the top with cream and a sprinkling of sugar. Bake in a 425° oven for 40 to 50 minutes or until top crust is browned. It's great served up with scoops of French vanilla ice cream.

KITSAP PENINSULA PUMPKIN PIE

2 eggs
1 1/2 cups cooked pumpkin
1 cup brown sugar
1/2 teaspoon salt
1/2 teaspoon cinnamon
1/2 teaspoon nutmeg
1/2 cup half and half
3 tablespoons sherry
1 unbaked pie shell

All you have to do is to beat the eggs lightly and combine with the other ingredients. Pour that sludge into the unbaked pie shell and bake for 10 minutes at 400°. Reduce oven heat to 350° and continue baking for 30 to 40 minutes or until the filling is well set.

WHIDBEY DESSERT CUPS

1 cup sugar
2/3 cup cocoa
2 teaspoons instant powdered coffee
1/3 cup water
4 egg yolks
10 maraschino cherries, stemmed and pitted
1 cup whipping cream
2/3 cup chopped semisweet chocolate
1/3 cup chopped toasted almonds

Sift the sugar, cocoa and powdered coffee into a pan and beat in the water with a whisk. Bring to a boil and stir-cook for 10 minutes until the sugar is dissolved and the gloop is smooth.

Beat the egg yolks at high speed in an electric mixer until fluffy. Reduce mixer speed to medium and add the hot chocolate glunk in a slow, steady stream. Keep beating until smooth, scraping the bottom and sides of the bowl. Then chill for an hour.

Whip cream in mixing bowl until it forms peaks. Stir a large spoonful of the whipped cream into the chocolate mixture. When it is absorbed, carefully fold in the rest of the cream plus the coarsely chopped semisweet chocolate and the almonds, taking care you don't reduce the whipped cream to a puddle.

Plunk 10 paper cups in a muffin pan. Fill a third of each cup with the chocolate cream mixture, toss in a cherry and add more chocolate mixture until the cup is two-thirds full.

Freeze for at least four hours, but the great thing about this dessert is that it will hold, covered by plastic wrap, in a freezer for a few weeks. Just plunk each one on a serving plate when it's time for dessert. You can either eat it straight or poof a bit of whipped cream atop each one.

BAINBRIDGE BARS

3/4 cup margarine
2/3 cup white sugar
2/3 cup brown sugar
1 egg
1 teaspoon vanilla
2 medium bananas, peeled and mashed
1 1/2 cups sifted all-purpose flour
1/2 cup rye flour
2 teaspoons baking powder
1/2 teaspoon salt
6 ounces walnuts

Cream together the margarine, white sugar and brown sugar until fluffy. Add the egg and vanilla and beat. Moosh in the mashed bananas.

Stir together the all-purpose flour and the rye flour, the baking powder and salt. Add to the banana gloop and beat again. Stir in nuts.

Spread banana mixture in a greased, 10-by-15-inch baking pan and shove into a 350° oven for 25 minutes or until done. Cool and cut into squares or bars.

CROSS-SOUND CAKE

1-pound, 2-ounce package yellow cake mix
3 3/4 ounce package instant French vanilla pudding mix
4 eggs
1 cup sour cream
1/2 cup vegetable oil
1/2 cup cream sherry
1/4 cup poppy seeds

In a large bowl moosh together all the ingredients except the seeds. Beat at medium speed for four minutes, scraping the sides of the bowl. Add the seeds and blend one minute more.

Pour this mess into a greased Bundt or angel food cake pan. Bake an hour at 350°, then cool the cake in the pan over a rack for 15 minutes. Turn the cake out onto a plate and let cool completely before cutting.

SHERRY PUDDING

1/4 cup sifted flour
1 cup sugar
1/2 teaspoon salt
1/2 teaspoon cinnamon
3 tablespoons sherry
2 tablespoons lemon juice
3 beaten egg yolks
1 cup milk (less 1 tablespoon)
2 stiffly beaten egg whites

Mix together the flour, sugar, salt and cinnamon in a bowl.

Stir in the sherry, lemon juice, egg yolks and milk. Fold in the beaten egg whites and pour this sludge into a 11/2-quart casserole. Set into a pan of water 1-inch deep and bake in a 350° oven for 25 to 30 minutes. Let cool to room temperature, then chill.

Serve in dessert glasses with brown sugar sauce and coarsely chopped toasted almonds over the top.

BROWN SUGAR SAUCE

Combine 1/2 cup of brown sugar and 1 1/2 tablespoons of flour. Add 1/4 cup each of cold water and dry white wine. Stir to make a smooth paste, then stir-cook (or cook-stir if you are left handed) over medium heat until it thickens. Stir in 1 1/2 tablespoons cream, 1/2 tablespoon butter, 1/4 teaspoon vanilla and a dash of salt. This dessert should serve four to six.

HAZEL'S APPLE CRISP

6 Granny Smith apples
1/2 cup sugar
juice of one lemon
1/2 teaspoon cinnamon

Peel, core and slice the apples. In a souvenir bowl from Champoeg State Park, mix the apples with the sugar, lemon juice and cinnamon. Plop this mess into a greased, 12-inch-by-9-inch casserole dish and sprinkle the following mixture over the top.

THE TOPPING

1 cup firmly packed brown sugar
1 cup white sugar
2/3 cup flour
1 stick butter
1 cup coarsely chopped hazelnuts
1 1/2 teaspoon crushed coriander seeds

Combine the sugars, flour and softened butter and cut with a pastry blender until you have a coarse meal. Add the nuts and coriander, mix again and scatter over the apples.

Bake the crisp in a 375° oven for 40 minutes and serve with whipped cream or French vanilla ice cream.

TEDDY'S TARTS

8 cooked tart shells
3 pints ripe strawberries
1/3 cup find granulated sugar
brandy
1 cup red currant jelly
whipped cream

You say you want to know where to get the tart shells? I bought them frozen and then baked them. If you want to muck around with pate brisee you're going to miss your ferry.

Hull the strawberries and toss in a bowl with the third of a cup of sugar and two tablespoons of brandy.

Next combine in a saucepan the jelly and two tablespoons more of the brandy. When the jelly has melted use this sludge to paint the insides of the tart shells.

Next fill the shells with the strawberries and top with the cream, which has been whipped with some sugar and brandy to taste.

Fiscally Sound Fish 47
Fish Stew Seattle 51
Flag Pavilion Ribs 88
Foster Island Fungi 67
Fourth Street Fajitas 98
Fremont Fettuccine 58
Fremont Minestrone 12

G

Garfield Goulash 92
Garlic Greenery 27
Garlic-Soy Satay 98
Gasworks Chili 17
Gingerbread 3
Goe Tuck Chowder 51
Gracious Living Lasagna 60
Green Lake Cabbage Soup 12
Greek Green Beans 28
Grits for Brunch 24
Gwen's Beef 'N Beans 63.

H

Ham Loaf 21
Hamlin Halibut 40
Happy Clams 43
Hazel's Apple Crisp 102
Herbed Halibut 40
Hen Fruit and Ham 23
Hing Hay Pork 96
Highlands Halibut Cheeks 39
Honolulu Ribs 88
Hot Chicken Salad 8

I

Indian Curry Casserole 96

J

Jackson Street Noodles 98
Java Gingerbread 3

K

King Street Salmon Steaks 39
King Street Teriyaki 95
Kitsap Peninsula Pumpkin Pie 101
Kotletki 97

L

Lake City Lamb Stew 75
Lake City Lasagna 59

Lakemont Loin 74
Lamb Shanks Parthenon 75
Lander Avenue Loaf 21
Latona Lentil Soup 11
Leary Avenue Loaf 64
Leftover Turkey Casserole 83
Lighthouse Eggs 22
Ling Cod Lopez 48
Lots of Lentil Soup 14
Louie's Seafood Salad Sauce 8
Loyal Heights Loaf 64

M

Madison Park Macaroni 58
Madrona Mushroom Sauce 67
Main Street Mein 97
Mama's Meatballs 64
Maple Syrup Chops 76
Mariner Ribs 88
Market Street Meatballs 63
Marmalade Ribs 87
Mashed Potato Ring 32
Mayonnaise, Basil 7
Meal from the Heart 80
Meatballs 63, 64
Meridian Broccoli Chowder 12
Minestrone 12
More Ballard Balls 63
Moss Point Macaroni 58
Muffins 4
Mushroom Chicken Chowder 11

N

No-Brown Sloth Stew 91
Noodles, Jackson Street 98
North Bend Beans 18

O

Oh Come All Ye Oysters Stew 43
Onion Soup 11
Orzo Soup 14

P

P and P Potatoes 31
Pacific Pork Loin 76
Pasquale's Peppers 74
Pasta Pepper Salad 7
Pat's Chupay 36
Perkin's Lane Pork 73
Phinney Potatoes 31
Pike Place Pea Salad 7

To order extra copies of
The Seattle Cookbook,
please send a check for $14.95 (tax included),
payable to the Seattle Post-Intelligencer to:

Public Affairs Department
Seattle Post Intelligencer
101 Elliott Avenue West
Seattle, Washington 98119